THE

BLUE PEARL

THE

BLUE PEARL

GETTING THE MOST
FROM COACHING

Shae Hadden

THE BLUE PEARL

ORDERING INFORMATION

Quantity Sales. Special discounts are available on quantity purchases by corporations, associations, and others. Visit shaehadden.com for details.
Individual Sales. This publication is available through Amazon.com in both print and e-book formats.

ISBN: 978-1492167822

Printed in the United States of America

First Edition, 2014

Copy editing Paula Sarson

Cover design Laurie Varga

Interior design Laurie Varga & Shae Hadden

AUTHOR'S NOTE

In some cases, coachees who participated in this book have opted to go by a pseudonym or to use only part of their name. I respect their right to privacy and believe that their anonymity in no way detracts from the value of their story. The actual events and circumstances depicted in my personal stories are as accurate as I could manage. Memory, however, is unstable, and interpretation personal. I have chosen to interpret all these events and circumstances in my life as learning opportunities. If you suspect otherwise, e-mail me at shae@shaehadden.com. I'll tell you if you're right…that is, if I even know myself.

To all those who choose to stand for the success
of another human being

And in loving memory of my mother

CONTENTS

FOREWORD by Jim Selman — xi

INTRODUCTION — xv

ONE: DESIRE — 1

Crises — 2

Dilemmas — 12

Transitions — 22

Self-Improvement — 32

Learning — 43

TWO: DESIGN — 53

Assumptions & Expectations — 54

Competency — 68

Commitments — 81

Discomfort — 94

Responsibility — 107

THREE: DISCOVER   120

Being   121

Respect   131

Patterns   142

Accountability   155

Power   168

EPILOGUE   184

ACKNOWLEDGMENTS   189

APPENDIX   191
Coaches Interviewed

NOTES   197

INDEX OF PEOPLE   201

ABOUT THE AUTHOR   205

FOREWORD

In 1983 my colleagues and I began to ask why it was that virtually all athletes and performing artists had more or less permanent relationships with a coach, while in business very few people even acknowledged the possibility of such a relationship. Those who could work with a coach were mostly viewed as "having a problem" and, generally, these individuals viewed a coach in the same context as they might consider an advisor or a consultant. When business hired coaches, they were usually from sports and were primarily working as motivational speakers.

This inquiry eventually led to our hosting a global videoconference of famous sports coaches (including George Allen from football, Red Auerbach and John Wooden from basketball, and Tim Gallwey from tennis) to explore the underlying principles and distinctions of coaching—regardless of the "game" or subject being coached. At that time, we focused on discovering with them what they all shared in common. We had no idea we were laying the foundation for an industry, that coaching would become a buzzword, or that coaching would become integrated in leadership development in all areas of society.

Since the publication of "Coaching and the Art of Management" in 1989, tens of thousands of individuals have declared themselves professional coaches, dozens of training and certification schools and several associations have grown in attempts to establish professional standards for coaching, a number of institutes and foundations have been set up to study and "legitimize" the profession, and most business executives have encountered or are working with a coach. This phenomenon has been chronicled in Dr. Vikki Brock's excellent dissertation "Grounded Theory of the Roots and Emergence of Coaching," which reveals the grounding and history of this emerging industry.

What has been missing until now are insights into why coaching is such a powerful element in modern business and organizations, what the coachee needs to bring to a coaching relationship to get maximum value from the process, and, most importantly, what in the *relationship* between a coach and a coachee contributes to effectiveness or shifts the way people view themselves and their world. In this book, Shae Hadden explores these questions and proposes some practical pathways for enhancing and empowering the coaching experience for anyone committed to achieving breakthroughs in performance.

The central idea this book suggests is that great coaching has as much or more to do with the commitment and personal responsibility of the coachee as it does the skill and techniques of a coach. In traditional management, power is vested in the authority and expertise of a manager. As we will see in the following pages, power in a coaching relationship is a function of the commitment of the person being coached combined with the possibility that the coach brings to their relationship.

In this sense, this book is about you and what your commitments are in your work and in your life. As I was reading it, I reflected that too often we "settle" for what is reasonable and predictable and we are blind to the possibility that through a relationship with someone else—a coach—we might achieve what we've failed to achieve on our own, even go far beyond whatever we think is possible. Shae shows us that coaching is not so much about maximizing results within our real or imagined limitations, but in redefining the boundaries of what is possible and transforming limitations into stepping-stones for success.

Before you begin reading, ask yourself, "What would I want to accomplish if I were not limited by whatever it is that I think limits me?"

I predict that by the time you've finished reading, not only will you be inspired by what is possible for you personally and for your organization, but also you will have either shifted the dynamic in the conversations with your existing coach (if you have one) or you will have the basis for finding and beginning to work successfully with a professional coach.

If you are a coach, this book can be a powerful reminder of the privilege to coach others and the gift they give us when they trust us with so much of their future. In addition, I suggest that, for many of us, this book can also give us insight into our own practices and why we're effective when we are. I am making *The Blue Pearl* required reading for those I coach in the future.

James (Jim) C. Selman
Ojai, CA
December 2013

INTRODUCTION

When we hire a coach, we are investing in our success. Our challenge as consumers lies in knowing how to make the most of that coaching investment.

Reading up on specific coaching methodologies, certification programs, and schools may be informative, but it won't guarantee you'll be able to make the right choice and get results from working with a coach. To be honest, when I first thought about having a coach for my business, my information gathering left me more confused than when I began. And after I had worked with a coach, I found it difficult to share my experience of being coached with others. They would look at me quizzically when I talked about why I thought I was getting value out of coaching when some of my colleagues weren't.

Like many professionals who help others, success for a coach shows up in the results their clients achieve. However, unlike other helping professions, coaching isn't about solving problems. Coaching, at its best, is about transforming your perspective for a specific purpose—so you can be in action, unimpeded by limiting beliefs and habitual patterns of thinking and doing, to achieve extraordinary results in the areas of life you care about most.

I know from personal experience that coaching works. Coaches have helped me in ways I couldn't anticipate or predict or even explain. But my perceptions and my belief about the workability of coaching were limited to just that—my experience. Curious about other people's perspectives and experiences, I began an inquiry that led to this book—an inquiry that revolved around two questions:

Why is it that some people experience extraordinary success working with a coach when others notice only incremental improvement?

What's working in successful coaching relationships?

The content for this book came from the many one-on-one conversations I had with coaches and coachees over the course of a year. No consensus emerged from my discussions. Instead, a rich diversity of perspectives led me away from a "model of success" and further into a search for areas where our conversations intersected. *What follows is not a formula.* What follows is a compilation of individual stories organized around common threads in the conversations I had with the people who were kind enough to engage in this inquiry with me.

The structure of this book reflects an overall unity that emerged from these diverse points of view. Each main section of the book focuses on an area critical to effective coaching:

- **DESIRE** | What brings people to coaching
- **DESIGN** | What coaches and coachees focus on when designing their coaching relationship
- **DISCOVER** | Where people look to get results from being coached.

Each chapter starts with a brief story from my life, followed by a coachee's story that relates to the same topic. Reflections and further insights I gained after speaking with a particular coachee and the related learning I gathered from all the coaches I interviewed close each chapter. My intentions were to respect the confidence of every coaching relationship and to *not* write an autobiography. And so coaches are quoted but not named in the coachees' stories. My personal stories do not appear in chronological sequence. They appear in an order that shows how I've grown and the process I've gone through in being coached over a period of ten years.

I leave it to you to draw your own conclusions—or develop your own perspective—on what will make coaching work for you and where you, too, may pay it forward. May this contribute to your success and the success of many others.

The will to win, the desire to succeed, the urge to reach your full potential…these are the keys that will unlock the door to personal excellence.

Confucius[1]

DESIRE

It is said that when the coachee is ready, the coach appears. And when the coach is ready, the coachee appears.

Desire brings coachee and coach together.

The coachee desires to have or do something they haven't been able to do yet in their life. Perhaps they want to resolve a dilemma they cannot seem to address on their own. Perhaps they long for objective help in dealing with life's little and not so little crises. Maybe they passionately desire to improve their performance, to master a skill, to learn. Sometimes they simply have a desire to be transformed by the presence of a master coach.

The coach desires to contribute the best of who they are to others.

Desire: the gateway to a vital, enlivening coaching relationship.

The journey begins here.

CRISES

The office door slams against my nose. I bend down to pick up my bags.

An out-of-control voice yells through the door at me, "And don't come back!"

I find myself wandering aimlessly through the park with my belongings, cold rain trickling down my neck, creeping between my toes, washing my face clean. I can't believe what just happened. My boss has been spying on my e-mails and this morning she accused me of not being trustworthy. Pointing to a message in which I expressed my concern about a direction we were considering on a project to one of the consultants we were working with, she told me to pack up my desk and leave.

In fact, I was genuinely worried that what had been proposed in my absence hadn't taken everything into account. My e-mail included a suggestion that we have a conversation about emerging industry trends. I was seeing a potential threat in the marketplace—new choices available to buyers that could negatively impact our client's sales.

I feel numb **and** raw simultaneously. I had just returned to the office after attending my mother's funeral. She died suddenly two weeks ago. And now I've been fired.

I know there's no going back. I'm not interested in fighting. I really

don't know what I'm interested in. I need to grieve these lo[...]
I have absolutely no idea what I'm going to do next.

So much for this career choice. Here we go—hitting bottom—again. I'm not getting any younger. What will I tell my husband? What will I tell my father? They say when one door closes, another opens. I'm not sure there will be many more doors for me. I wish I had a different life. I'm a serial failure. I wish I was someone else.

There goes the little voice in my head again, droning on and on.

I wish some other voice—any other voice—was whispering in my ear.

More than a decade has passed since that rainy walk in the park.

Being fired shook my world. I can still remember how trapped and alone I felt. In the heat of the moment, I didn't recognize the crisis as a crisis. I felt as if I had no choice in the matter. That evening, I could see I'd reached a major turning point, but I believed there was nothing I could have done differently.

As a singer, I'd been coached most of my life. When I gave up performing and went into the business world, I gave up being coached as well. But that evening, lying awake staring at the ceiling while my husband slept soundly beside me, I began to long for someone objective whom I could count on to help me with the new challenges I'd created for myself.

We can't predict the future. I couldn't have foreseen that one door slamming shut so loudly would quietly open the door to coaching again and to a whole field of new possibilities. That one walk in the park would lead to working with a masterful executive coach, interviewing almost one hundred coaches and coachees over the course of a year, researching coaching methodologies and approaches, completing a professional coaching program, and talking informally with all kinds of people about their experiences of being coached. Or that, one day, I might realize that many of my persistent questions about being coached and how to get the most out of

; other people wanted answered as well. I predicted you'd be reading these words.

) get the most out of your coaching ith you what I've learned about coaching ersations—what it is and what it isn't, when it at makes it work. As you read the following consider not only what these people have achieved with coaching, but also what they created in their coaching relationship that supported their success.

MEETING PAOLO

As I sit here listening to Paolo begin to tell me his story, I can feel knots of tension forming in my neck and shoulders. That's because he's telling me about the moment he knew he was on the verge of losing his job. Our bodies instinctively remember how to respond to a threatening crisis. Fight, freeze, or flee. All those years ago, I fled from being fired and then I went into fight mode. That seemed to work…for a while. But that incessant little voice in my head truly screwed things up for me.

Refocus, Shae. Come back to Paolo in this moment. He had the benefit of working with a coach when things fell apart, and I'm curious to know what it's like having that support. Paolo's words begin to seep into my awareness again and I start to extract the essence of his story.

> Paolo had just stepped into a new position as a national General Manager in a renowned multinational food company. Like many high achievers, he had a long history of successes and consistently superior performance. But within the first week, he was facing an unanticipated quality crisis. Not a problem. Paolo dug in, pulling out all the stops and working 24/7 towards turning things around. But the company lost 20 percent of their turnover in the next few months. He was under enormous pressure and stress to deliver extraordinary results, yet he couldn't see a yard ahead of himself.

No matter what he did, he sensed he was going nowhere fast.

And then a message arrived that changed everything. His daughter was facing a potentially life-threatening medical crisis. Suddenly, his family became a priority.

Paolo urgently needed to manage the critical problems he was facing in his career and family life. He was open to anything, to anyone who could help him. Paolo's boss recommended he meet with an executive coach. Specifically, a masterful coach who had a reputation for helping leaders transform not only their performance, but also their entire life. Great. A coach could focus immediately on problem solving these critical issues and then work with him on planning for the future.

Luckily, Paolo's boss recognized the value of coaching for him at this point in his life. Having someone to help with problem solving would have worked for me.

But Paolo was somewhat surprised by what happened next. His coach started rigorously working with him on clarifying his purpose—both professionally and personally. He invited Paolo to look beyond the immediate crises and to imagine himself in the future. To consider what he wanted to experience in life, what contributions he wanted to make, and who he wanted to be.

Once he had a clear vision of himself in the future, Paolo's coach invited him to think about times in the past when he had achieved outstanding results. And then to reflect on who he was being in those moments. Paolo recalled when he had been accepted at a renowned university that had a reputation for extremely high standards. He remembered when he had won a coveted position as a trainee with one of the world's greatest consumer goods companies. In both cases, he saw a man who was confident, clear about his priorities and his vision, fully committed, without doubt about his capacity to play through to his endgame.

Hm. I expected coaching would focus on solving urgent problems first. I wonder where this is going.

Paolo also remembered times of mediocre results—times when he had been doubtful, when he had lacked a clear vision, and when he hadn't pushed himself to raise the bar and go beyond his comfort zone.

With this insight into the importance of who he was being, Paolo chose to take the stand that, no matter what happened, he would be able to deal with it. Instead of seeing what was happening in the present as problems to be fixed, he saw them as opportunities to define the kind of leader and family man he wanted to be, what he valued, and what he wanted to accomplish in his life.

The newly envisioned future he had created for himself became the context for all his choices and actions—a context that helped him become stronger, more serene, more mature in traversing life's tough spots. Paolo tells me that, thinking in this long-term way about his endgame at work and at home, he found his circumstances morphed from problems of great significance into hurdles to be overcome on his path to success.

I wonder what it would be like to relate to life in that way. I assume it would be less stressful.

Thus began their coaching. After the immediate health issue with his daughter subsided, Paolo began to look more closely at how others perceived him as a leader. He started by asking for feedback from each of his direct reports during his company's annual performance evaluation process.

"When I finished each evaluation, I gave people an opportunity to give *me* direct feedback—with the condition that I would just listen and not speak. I didn't need to justify my actions: *what was relevant was their perceptions.* I learned that most of the time when someone gave me negative feedback, I had been trying to do what they said but I hadn't been doing it very well. It was perceived totally differently from my intention. *It was my job to fix how I acted.*"

Paolo

When my boss gave me negative feedback for that e-mail, I tried to justify my actions by explaining my intentions in the hope that she would perceive me positively. Trying to prove I was "right" in doing what I did in the way I did backfired. We both ended up on the defensive, resisting each other. That explosive ending to our relationship has always bothered me. It was not the result I had intended.

> Paolo started experimenting. He modified his actions until they more closely delivered the outcomes he intended. He began to create his life in such a way that he could manage his commitments at work *and* have time and energy for his family. He generated a new game for himself and for his team to play at work: focused, committed effort towards aggressive goals *without sacrifice.*

> He shifted away from being a senior executive intent on executing everything himself. He built his team so that he could delegate to them and know they would deliver results. This shifted everyone's choices and actions. The ever-present hallway conversation about work/life balance disappeared. Everyone now knows it's possible to produce unpredictable results without having to stay in the office after 6 p.m. every night.

Now *this* I want to experience!

> Within a year, Paolo's colleagues were describing him in terms of "empowerment," "serenity," "inspiration," "a leader with a clear endgame who makes wise decisions." For Paolo, coaching was transformative.

"What's changed is me. Most of the people, including my boss, told me with some amazement that I was being a different man. I was clearly being a different person. It was not a question of evolution: it was a major transformation."

Paolo

Transformation. Not problem solving. A marked change in who he was being. I wonder how this plays out over time.

Another major challenge awaited Paolo. One of the world's largest multinational beverage companies decided to sue him personally. Faced with the possibility of losing everything, Paolo turned to his coach. He needed to find a perspective that could help him deal with the fear of being challenged in this way.

Paolo knew he was not guilty. Acknowledging that the lawsuit was not personal helped alleviate *some* of his stress, but not all. It was impossible to avoid the presence of the multinational's brand in his life: everywhere he looked, there they were. The sight of their advertisements and products only fuelled his anxiety and anger.

With his coach's ongoing support, Paolo was able to ride the wave of the legal action with some equanimity, while continuing the cycles of his own development as a leader and a human being. At his coach's suggestion, Paolo chose to stop resisting what was happening, to stop using all his energy fighting and worrying about what could happen to his reputation and his life if the lawsuit were successful. Instead, he opted to live in integrity and ease.

"You have to realize over time whether you're transforming or not. I find that whenever I make a transformation and I feel really great, it's followed by a time when I feel like I'm at a dead end. As if I'm in a dark room and I don't see any more doors and I wonder, 'Where do I go next?' I'm aware that I don't know everything, but I can't see it. Whenever I say to my coach, 'I'm not evolving anymore and I don't know where to go next,' I don't know why but a door opens and I discover a completely new room. And I work on that room until everything becomes dark again. And eventually the next room appears."

Paolo

Paolo sounded happy and serene as he described how the last few years have been the best of his life. Instead of fighting the lawsuit head-on, he let it run its course. He emerged unscathed and cleared of all charges. He doesn't get overly stressed at work anymore. He has been performing even better than when he joined the company as a high-potential leader. His career has been extraordinary. Every year, he has received promotions and the maximum bonuses possible.

And he continues to give away the best of what he has received from his coach to help others in their journey.

New problems and crises may be, as Paolo called them, simply "hurdles" to be overcome. And they may also be opportunities for further transformation. The coaching Paolo experienced didn't leave him with a one-shot solution to a problem. It left him transformed— and in a continuing process of transformation.

REFLECTING

Talking with Paolo about his experience of coaching left me with some strong initial impressions.

Effective coaching delivers results. Not just any results. Results that count for the coachee in the things that matter most to them. With coaching, Paolo was able to achieve what he was committed to achieving with his career and his family that he couldn't accomplish by himself.

Successful coachees are a request for coaching. They're not looking for coaching in just a "sounds like a good idea" kind of way, but in a no-holds-barred, "let's get this done" kind of way. Paolo came to his coach like this, ready and wanting to be coached. And it was clear to me in the way he spoke that he was authentically committed not only to his own success, but also to the success of his coach in coaching him. In speaking with very experienced coaches, they echoed this idea that demand and commitment form part of the context of effective coaching relationships.

> "Coaching only occurs in the presence of a demand for it. I can't coach you if you don't want to be coached. What we're here to do is work together to produce a state change in your performance. I can't do it *to* you. I can't do it *for* you. I can only do it *with* you."
>
> Chris Majer, Human Potential Project

Coaching makes transformation possible. It may not be what we're looking for when we hire a coach, but as we can see with Paolo, a state change is possible.

Transformative coaching starts with looking at the future you're living into. Designing a different future, a new story to live into, shifts how you see and relate to yourself, other people, your circumstances, time. That shift in perspective fundamentally changes everything. It gives you new ways of responding to crises, new possibilities for action, better performance, and new results. It's like lining yourself up for success.

New Future ⇨ New Perspective ⇨ New Relationships ⇨
New Possibilities ⇨ New Actions ⇨
Better Performance ⇨ Desired Results

Coaching isn't about "fixing" us. We may come into coaching assuming we're "broken" and that we need a coach to help put us back together again so we can achieve the results we want. But coaches stand for their coachees being "whole" as they are. They help us shift our perspective so we can begin to see ourselves with some sense of curiosity and appreciation. They tap into our innate capacities to imagine, to create, to learn, to grow, and to generate what we want in the world. They may also work with us to develop whatever competencies we need so we can perform at higher levels and accomplish what we set out to do.

INTEGRATING

I sense that these four ideas imply a change we may need to be willing to make to get the most out of coaching. **Realizing the results we want may involve letting go of our old stories about what's possible for us and who we are.** My solo performer mindset, for example, has me playing the superhero in business, constantly trying to prove myself, trying to solve problems alone. I may need to give up the belief that I can succeed by myself.

This has me passionately asking two questions now:

What *is* coaching?

What is it in a coaching relationship that supports transformation and results?

DILEMMAS

Standstill.

The place where uncertainty reigns supreme. A point of stuckness where "Stop" is better than "Go." Where willpower is powerless.

Whenever I've spent long periods in this place, I find myself unconsciously creating holding patterns—behaviors and recurring thoughts—that further entrench me in my feeling stuck. Frenetic activity masks my inability to decide. Until I realize what's happening and come to a standstill.

After being fired, I have absolutely no idea what to do.

Resignation hangs out on my doorstep. Creative thinking, new ideas, the innovations I need to become unstuck elude me.

I cannot see the "million ways" to look at my current situation or the million ways to resolve it.

Even when I do see the glimmer of a way, I'm unable or reluctant to choose it. Experience tells me that sometimes, when I do choose, my actions don't resolve my problem. I end up stuck with solutions that don't work or outcomes that are less than desirable. In choosing, I may even end up causing harm to myself or others. Or I may be faced with a choice I don't want to have to make between my ethics and making a living.

I find myself becoming increasingly anxious, borderline fearful. I can't tell my husband that I anticipate being left with no one and nothing—no matter what course of action I choose in this moment. Suck it up, my inner superhero says. Find an answer to the problem of "no income" and "no job prospects."

Yet I'm getting nowhere. In my mind, I make the same connections over and over again between possible solutions and their consequences. I feel as if I'm caught in a closed loop, seeing things the same way I always have.

I'm a failure looking forward to a future of more failures. No matter what I choose, my life is just not going to be workable.

My incessant internal monologue saps my energy and makes it difficult to make even the most basic choices. I'm overwhelmed. The little voice inside my head tells me to stop. The safest choice right now is to *do nothing*.

But I know that choice, too, can lead to disaster.

MEETING NIGEL

A decade later, I'm in sunny San Francisco at a fund-raising luncheon. A brief introduction to CEO Nigel Bennett ends with a promise to connect for a conversation in our shared home city. And now, here I am, sitting beside the landmark green Vespa that decorates the Vancouver café where we've chosen to meet. We're talking about our shared concerns and what we're up to in the world. I discover that Nigel has experienced his fair share of dilemmas as an entrepreneur and businessman—and that his executive coach has played a key role in helping him get "unstuck." I'm all ears.

> Nigel was frustrated. He believed it was possible to have tremendous business success along with a fulfilling and satisfying lifestyle. It's true, his company, Aqua-Guard Spill Response Inc., was doing very well providing oil recovery equipment and services to organizations around the world. But, as with many businesses, there were some problems that seemed to perpetuate themselves, no matter what solutions he came up with.
>
> He was in the shower every morning, anxiously thinking about what unanticipated crisis he'd have to deal with that day, or how he was going to make payroll, or who he was going to have to lay off. He was experiencing high blood pressure and some other

inexplicable health symptoms. And, like many business owners with a young family, he didn't want to make the mistake of working so hard that he missed the opportunity to spend time with his children as they grew up.

Success has dilemmas—just as failure does. Interesting.

Nigel found that all the ways he had been coping with and managing his circumstances were no longer working for him. The longer the dilemmas in his business and life went unresolved, the more often he found himself thinking of walking away from it all to go sell T-shirts on the beach.

As a responsible business owner, husband, and father, he chose to do the next best thing. He recognized that the way he had been thinking about his problems wasn't solving them, and that he couldn't get outside his own thinking—he couldn't see beyond his own perspective—alone. He turned to a trusted advisor, who referred him to a business coach specializing in working with CEOs and entrepreneurs.

At first, Nigel brought a healthy skepticism to the coaching relationship. He began by looking to his coach for advice on the specific issues he wanted to address. He quickly found out that coaching can be much more than having access to an expert's opinion on the best solution to a problem. It can be about discovering things for yourself, with your coach's help and prompting. And in the process of discovering your own answers, you can see how your habitual ways of thinking about things contribute to the persistence of dilemmas.

I sense strength and humility in Nigel as he tells me this, as well as his unspoken commitment to being responsible for the success of his business and the well-being of his employees and clients. As a sole proprietor, I can only imagine what it must be like being responsible for the future of so many others.

Nigel's coach first invited him to create a mind map of all the issues in his life where he assessed something was unresolved or stuck. The picture he drew looked like a massive meteor field, with numerous huge boulders floating among many little rocks. Nigel's next mission was to look at the facts: what issues had built up over the years, the story he had about each one, any connections between issues, and his current circumstances.

With this information, he began to identify and prioritize what he could do each month to clear away some of the smaller meteors. Nigel's coach played an important part in helping him think about his thinking and in keeping him on track in this process.

"My coach would hold me accountable to get things done. That really helped in the beginning. Being a CEO, I'm not really accountable to anyone but myself. You really get a lot done when you isolate what's most important to you, see what diversions you're creating that pull you away from dealing with things you don't want to deal with, and have someone holding your feet to the fire."

Nigel Bennett, Co-founder/Principal,

Aqua-Guard Spill Response Inc.

The CEO shares the same challenge as the sole proprietor: no one to be accountable to but yourself. So when you have no boss and find yourself stuck and distracted, a coach can help keep you focused on what's most important to you.

Persistence and tenacity played an important part in this "honeymoon phase" of the coaching relationship. As Nigel's smaller issues were taken care of in the first few months, he came face-to-face with some larger meteors that he believed weren't going to be as easy to address. He was aware that looking at everything and dealing with whatever might come up would take more time and cost more money. But quitting would leave Nigel with major issues and dilemmas unresolved.

Big issues (including unresolved conflicts) that I've walked away from have always found a way of coming back to haunt me. Avoiding what's difficult can drag out our dilemmas interminably and keep us stuck.

Nigel chose to keep on going with his coach, rather than succumb to fear and quit. From that point on, every subsequent coaching session, without fail, helped develop more trust and understanding between them. As Nigel let down his guard and opened up more about his dilemmas, his coach began to help him learn how to have the difficult conversations necessary for his well-being and the future of his company. Over time, Nigel found that a steadfast approach of rigorously examining his thinking, trying out new ways of responding to problems, and taking care of increasingly larger issues actually minimized many bigger issues until they eventually disappeared altogether.

But life doesn't stop happening just because we're working on our dilemmas with a coach. As crisis after crisis presented itself in his business, Nigel took advantage of them as opportunities to master staying focused on what was most important as a leader: identifying critical issues, breaking them down, deciding what needs to be done, and acting. From dealing with embezzlement to firing people and then handling negotiations for a potential acquisition, he found himself becoming more confident, settled, and optimistic about the future.

Nigel has paused. I wait for a moment, then look up from studying the edge of my coffee cup. He's looking at me and I can tell he's wondering whether to stop there. I wait in silence until he leans forward and continues.

One large meteor remained: a troublesome relationship from the past that seemed to hover in the center of his life. A relationship that impacted both his business and his well-being.

Many years earlier, Nigel had discovered that a trusted colleague in his inner circle had been lying to him for many years. At the time, he had broken off the relationship abruptly and set course in another direction. Now, having worked through most of his minefield with his coach, Nigel was ready to look at the heart of any lingering issues he had around trust and respect—core values that are intrinsic to who he is as a businessman and father.

At his coach's suggestion, Nigel inquired further to find out what the facts actually were around this person's choices and actions. And then he initiated a conversation with the individual who had lied to him to hear their perspective about what had happened.

Talk about a difficult conversation!

Rather than challenge or resist what the person said, Nigel chose to just listen, noting where their version of the truth varied from the facts. The story they told ended with a request for help in dealing with the consequences of a lie they had told someone else. Acknowledging that this person had to grow up and be responsible for cleaning up their own messes, Nigel turned down the request and made it clear he was only interested in maintaining relationships based in honesty and integrity.

A coach would be a wonderful resource to call on for help in preparing for that meeting.

"You can't necessarily sit down with the people in your business or your close personal friends and discuss *everything* in your life. You can only take certain things so far with each of them. Working with a coach has helped me with everything I've been able to do and accomplish over the past twenty years—including balancing my life and keeping my family together. Over time, my coach and I have evolved together."

Nigel Bennett

Confronting our dilemmas can make a substantial difference to our performance, whether we're already a high-performing leader, a successful entrepreneur, or someone starting over again. I look at Nigel and know that learning how to courageously and steadfastly address issues—lingering unresolved problems or new dilemmas—has contributed to developing the courageous leader sitting before me.

> Nigel smiles and settles back into his seat. He tells me that not only has his blood pressure returned to normal, but he has regained a new balance in his life. He now has time to be a father to his teenage children: he's involved with them in helping nonprofit organizations build homes for the homeless and advocating for the rights of indigenous peoples and nature. His company is set on a steady course with trusted partners at the helm. As we wrap up our conversation, this highly successful entrepreneur is already in motion, heading out the door to catch the next SeaBus and already turning his attention to his next adventure.

REFLECTING

In speaking with Nigel and then later with his coach, I think I'm beginning to get a sense of what coaching is and what makes it work.

Coaching is a collaboration to face the tough stuff. Nigel and his coach focused on efficiently navigating the biggest obstacles he faced. Neither of them had the "answers," but together they figured it out by using an iterative process: identifying issues, making intentional choices, Nigel taking action, observing his results precisely, and adjusting appropriately.

> "It's much easier to keep yourself buried in work than it is to work towards your purpose."
>
> Kevin Lawrence, SGI Synergy Group Inc.

Coaching can help replace circular thinking and coping strategies with more productive activities like exploring, inventing, and moving into action. Success can come from brainstorming and testing out different ideas together, seeing what worked, discarding what didn't, and staying with the process.

Effective coaching engages your curiosity and desire to learn. Coaching is not consulting. Your coach doesn't analyze your situation to come up with answers to your problems. Their curiosity into where you're stuck and what has you stuck—whether that's unconscious or competing values, beliefs, demands, and commitments—can ignite your own curiosity and desire to learn.

> "A consultant is hired for their subject matter expertise. They're intervening in the observer / action / results cycle where they're prescribing a different action to the same observer. They're offering a solution that exists before you encounter the problem. Like prescriptive medicine. Coaching is working with the observer to support learning."
>
> Mark Cappellino, Primary Leadership LLC

Ultimately, great coaches do not want you to become dependent on them. They intend to help you learn and develop so you can deal with future challenges and dilemmas yourself. To that end, coaching can involve trying out different ways of observing the world and mastering new distinctions, practices, and competencies.

Great coaches get who you are and focus on what you want to achieve. The spotlight rests on you. Being committed to your commitments, they're fascinated with who you are and see you in ways you're not even aware of and may not even know how to articulate. They consciously relate to you as being intelligent, creative, and resourceful, while also seeing your strengths, habits, and limiting beliefs.

"My role as a coach is to help a person really understand who they are, what makes them tick, what they're passionate about…and then to set up their life and their business in a way that energizes and sustains them."

Kevin Lawrence

The commitment of great coaches begins and ends with having you win at the game you are playing. So they also look with you at your game and what's on your playing field.

Coaches separate facts from stories and remain objective. They guide you in distinguishing the facts of what's happening and what's happened in your game from your stories and interpretations. Feeling stuck and overwhelmed by my dilemma, for instance, is a sure sign that I'm attached to my story about who I am and what's possible for me in my current situation. My perspective has reached its limit of usefulness.

"A coach is somebody who really *'gets'* you. But they don't just get you as a product of your history. They get you as the *possibility* that is opened up by your commitments."

Don Arnoudse, The Arnoudse Group LLC

Although Nigel's coach could see the world through Nigel's eyes, have compassion for what he felt, and empathize with what he was experiencing, he himself did not get "stuck" in Nigel's story with him. Great coaches do not buy into your perspective or the way you've interpreted things or the drama you have created around how difficult your life is and why things should be different than the way they are.

Coaches create value and take risks in the coaching relationship. To serve you, a coach will help you look at what you've avoided, see what you have not seen, and do what you have not done. They may challenge you to drop any attachment to who you think you are and what "should" be happening, let go of the drama of your dilemmas and crises, and try on different points of view.

INTEGRATING

After listening to Paolo and Nigel, it sounds like coaches who effectively partner with you—who become a trusted ally on your journey—can help you transform dilemmas and crises into opportunities for growth and transformation.

Now what is it that distinguishes a coach as partner?

> The greatest good you can do for another is not just to
> share your riches, but to reveal to him his own.
>
> Benjamin Disraeli[1]

TRANSITIONS

My body doesn't work right now. I'm more dead than alive.

I'm not expert at troubleshooting physical breakdowns, so I call my doctor for help. She's not available and I'm rapidly getting worse. Off to emergency at the hospital. Three hours later, the doctors have a working diagnosis. A couple of looks under the hood and they identify the source of my problem and have a recommendation about how to solve it. Post-op infection: antibiotics under supervision for forty-eight hours. Two days later, I'm leaving the hospital, more alive than dead, and contemplating what other learning I can take away from this experience. I just wish someone could give me something that would help me get through my career transition this quickly and easily.

I know business—like life—is not necessarily an easy ride. I don't count on being rescued or having someone else "fix" or "solve" what is not working for me. What I do with my career—what I do with my life—is entirely up to me.

It's just that sometimes life throws us too many curve balls at once: health, career, finances, relationships all in turmoil simultaneously. Some days it seems like my problems are bigger than I am. Colleagues remind me to be a warrior, to "suck it up" and get on with it. They tell me what they'd do if they were me. They prod me to be in action. Their "Just do it" philosophy and well-intentioned advice doesn't help.

What I've been doing hasn't delivered the results I want. No leads. No prospects. No work. I don't know what to do next. Each day is more of an effort than the last.

I can't see what's standing in the way of my success. I don't know what questions to ask myself that will give me different answers from the ones I already have. I can't see my skills, my career, my life from any other perspective than my own. And I don't want to rely on someone else's answers to my problems.

I need to find my own way through this. Yet trying to find it alone isn't working.

It's time for some help.

MEETING VICTORIA

Some of my older female friends had warned me about the trials and tribulations of midlife. But it wasn't until my call today with Victoria that I can see for myself that I'm now standing fully in the middle of my midlife transition. Being fired was just the beginning of the middle. As I settle into my chair, phone in hand, I find myself being drawn further into her story. Even though we live in different countries, grew up in different cultures, and have followed different career paths, I see parallels between her life and my own.

> After twenty-five years, Victoria Jamison knew that her chosen career as a practicing psychotherapist was no longer serving her or her clients. She was feeling burned out, even though she'd moved away from a straightforward therapeutic model towards equine-assisted therapy combined with transformational coaching.

> Her personal journey was mirroring her professional journey: her twenty-year marriage had recently blown up, her finances were in challenging mode, and she was looking to relocate herself to a new home elsewhere in the state. Time to find someone who could help her create something new and fresh so she could move with relative grace through this transition out into the world.

> Aware of her own prejudice towards psychology and her desire to go deep to embrace both the richness of light and dark in herself,

she wanted to work with a coach familiar with the therapeutic model. A coach who could also keep her focused on being in action and moving forward in the world. Someone who had breadth and depth.

"I always thought of therapy, for better or for worse, like the mother: filling in, shoring up, nurturing. Coaching is like the father, helping the person out into the world."

Victoria Jamison, Licensed Clinical Social Worker /
Equine Experiential Therapist

This really hits home. What I needed coming out of the hospital was someone to help me "out into the world." Someone to help me figure out how to create a new life from the mess I found myself in.

Victoria decided to search for a transformational coach who could meet her where she was in her life. Specifically, a professional who was well trained in focusing on people's strengths, building on potential and experience, and delivering results. One of the certified coaches she was referred to combined a reputation for successfully integrating psychology, somatics, and equine-assisted therapy with an extensive knowledge of literature and myth, spirituality, Buddhism, and wisdom traditions. This broad understanding of the human condition and the fact that she had also transitioned from therapy to coaching herself could add a powerful dimension to their coaching relationship right from the start.

And what Victoria found interesting was that they started their coaching relationship before she officially engaged this professional as her coach. The coach offered and recommended to Victoria that they have two complimentary sessions before they make a commitment to each other. Since homework would be integral to their work together, Victoria found herself completing assignments even before she had hired a coach. The assignments related to the outcomes she wanted to produce. Completing the homework consistently revealed not only her commitment to the process, but also a bit about her thinking and mindset. Paying careful attention to the coaching relationship in this way at the beginning helped clarify the focus of their work together, ensured they were a good "fit," and began an iterative process of co-creating their partnership that they maintained throughout their journey.

"Coaches and therapists look at a lot of the same stuff, but they do it from different sides of the river. Therapy, like 12-step programs, is based on a pathological model that focuses on study and diagnosis to resolve issues. Coaching is based on a potentials and strengths model that focuses on empowering people to be in action."

Victoria Jamison

Victoria had already invested a lot of time and energy into knowing herself before she began working with her coach. That work had been invaluable and would be a rich resource she could draw on. But there's a difference between knowing one's self and being in action.

Here's one place where Victoria and I differ: a decade ago I had no problem being in action, but I'm not sure I even knew who I was. Interesting that either situation doesn't work. Seems we need to master both being ourselves and being in action—and perhaps in that order. Victoria had stopped talking, so I asked her in what area of her life she had stopped moving forward.

Victoria quietly shared that she had been trying to start a new career in equine-assisted therapy for a decade. She'd bought the domain name for her business five years in, but hadn't put up a website yet. She had taken some training, but was uncertain whether she needed more or whether she already knew everything she needed to get started.

Victoria's coach began to help her sort through these unresolved aspects of her life. No stranger to hard core struggle, pain, and suffering, this coach intuitively pulled different tools from her tool kit to help Victoria learn how to develop a skillful relationship with herself and her circumstances. Instead of feeling *or* acting in any given moment, Victoria learned how to be able to feel *and* act at the same time. Instead of thinking things had to be either one way *or* another, she learned how to integrate what might appear to be polar opposites and create a third possibility for herself. Instead of sabotaging herself with her thinking, she began to move out of her head and listen to the wisdom of her body.

Wisdom of the body. When everything in my life was falling apart, my body said, "Quit!" I briefly mention to Victoria my multiple trips to the hospital and the uncertainty of being a "medical mystery" to the doctors for several years. We connect for a moment around dealing with uncertainty…and then she calmly continues.

Her coach had told her about the "quitting phenomenon" when they first started working together. People often try coaching for a short period of time and then suddenly quit. It's like that moment when husband and wife realize the honeymoon has ended: both people have gotten to know each other intimately and the real work of the relationship begins. In coaching, that's when we run up against our own natural resistance to change. Anticipating that Victoria would come up against this, her coach talked to her about what it would look like when they got there, how they could respect her resistance, and how they could compassionately navigate this and future breakdowns together.

No wonder my midlife is turning out to be messy and painful. Resistance can show up even when we *want* change. Good intentions aren't enough. We need to overcome our resistance—however and whenever it shows up—to make the transition.

As a recovering alcoholic, Victoria knew that you can work the insights of the twelve steps as much as you want. But at some point, each step takes you and comes up and through your body. You physically embody what you need to learn.

For eight years, she had been living with a debilitating chronic pain condition. She had tried applying all the tools of psychoanalytic therapy to her condition—without success. Her pain was presenting her with an unequalled opportunity for learning.

"I was very identified with being a recovering addict and the whole pathology model. I was always coming from healing what's wrong, instead of moving forward in terms of what's right."

Victoria Jamison

Working somatically with her coach, Victoria first learned how to be with the feelings of pain without trying to control them. She became aware that whenever she focused on her thoughts or her words, her pain would remain intense and persist. Whenever she focused on what her body was saying, she could relax her muscles and breathe into the pain. This would often reduce the intensity of the feelings she was experiencing. Once she became aware of this connection between her thoughts and her physical experience, she could choose whether to make changes in the moment to alleviate it. Pain became her barometer as to whether or not she was present with her body.

I cannot believe how closely this mirrors my own experiences with chronic pain and mindfulness practices. The biggest breakthrough in healing came when I shifted my focus from fixing what was wrong with me to being present in the moment with whatever was happening. That shift made it possible for me to believe my future could be different than my past, that I could transition into a new life. Perhaps it was so for Victoria too.

It's been two years since Victoria began this transformational journey with her coach. Her chronic pain is now about 10 percent of what it used to be. Her website is up. She has all the training she needs. She has navigated her midlife passage with relative grace, emerging with the confidence that she can and will continue to be successful in her work and her life.

REFLECTING

After talking with Victoria, I wanted to know more about the differences between coaching and therapy and why we would turn to one or the other for help. What emerged in my conversations with professional coaches, including several who are both trained therapists and coaches, was a clear distinction between the two.

The context of therapy is "fixing": the focus is on healing the past. Therapy is about remedying past traumas or solving personality or behavioral "problems" so we can be fully present in life with some sense of well-being. In the therapeutic paradigm, there is something wrong with a client that needs to be "fixed."

Therapeutic interventions explore the question of *why* you're experiencing "dis-ease" today. This pathological model focuses on treating problems buried in the psyche and on controlling emotions and manipulating behaviors so you are *ready to play* your game.

> "Therapy is about unpacking the past and coming to some sense of understanding and peace about it. Coaching is really an opportunity to design your future—to look at what ways of being and acting generate the life you want."
>
> Nancy Miriam Hawley, Enlignment, Inc.

The context of coaching is learning: the focus is on being in action to create the future. Coaching is about helping individuals **clarify, design, and play** their game. In the coaching paradigm, no one and nothing needs "fixing." The coaching approach focuses on shifting individuals' perceptions of themselves, their path, and their playing field so they can take different actions—actions that produce the results they desire.

Coaching engagements explore the questions of **who, what, and when**. The coach focuses on pulling for something extraordinary from each player, asking them to go beyond what they believe are their personal limits to do what they have never done before.

> "Coaching is a client-led process and a relationship that is dedicated to the creation of something in the client's future—whether that's a business, a relationship, or an internal state of contentment or happiness. The relationship is in service of producing something that's relevant to the future they want to be in."
>
> Jennifer Cohen, Seven Stones Leadership Group LLC

With this distinction, I can also see that coaching is not for everyone at all times.

Coaches partner with "game-ready" players. Almost all the coaches I have spoken with try to assess up front whether a prospective client is really "game-ready" and committed to mastering their game and engaging fully on the playing field. That's not to say therapy is a prerequisite for coaching. It's just not always clear at the start whether someone will benefit best from coaching or therapy. People who have pervasive issues, such as cognitive or emotional filters that affect everything they see and impact every interaction they have, may not reveal their underlying coping strategies early on in a coaching relationship. They may very well be blind to them. However, coping strategies take tremendous energy to sustain. Since coaching focuses on helping people see themselves and their relationship to their game more clearly, coaches sometimes find themselves disclosing these adaptive behaviors later in the coaching process. It benefits everyone when coaches take responsibility for what they see and openly discuss with their clients whether therapy or coaching or some combination of the two will best serve their needs moving forward.

"As a therapist, I deal with the whole range of problems in people's lives: their relationships with their children, their spouses, their anxiety, depression, all the range of human distress. Alfred Adler called the last part of the psychotherapeutic process coaching. In Hebrew, the word for 'coaching' and 'training' is the same word. So to train people to new behaviors is the last stage of a treatment. As a coach, people come to me to achieve goals, to fulfill dreams, to make the best of themselves. They may have gone to therapy before and come up with a career or business idea they want to realize: it warms them to do something with the insights they now have about themselves to really do better, feel better, live better. To fulfill themselves."

Anabella Shaked, The Adler Institute, Israel

Great coaches are committed listeners who bring their whole selves to coaching. They can discern the emotions behind our words. They can hear what we're not saying that's influencing our mood. They can see where our thinking limits or stops us. And when we run up against our resistance to change, they keep listening for and speaking to our greatness. They can reconnect us to our bodies, our strengths, and our potential when we're in transition.

INTEGRATING

Life transitions can have us running for cover. Yet the only way out is through.

When it comes to my transitions, I want to work with a coach who will have genuine compassion for me as a human being and who will help me grow. Not someone who will dish out canned answers or conventional wisdom like some kind of recipe for success. I want to connect with a coach who I know respects *my* wisdom and is committed to helping me improve myself in whatever ways I need to realize my dreams.

Is it too much to expect my coach to be able to see what I need to learn to succeed?

> It's what you learn after you know it all that counts.
>
> John Wooden[1]

SELF-IMPROVEMENT

Ever since grade school, I've had a strong desire to succeed. I do the work—whatever it is—and I do it well. I'm well-organized, manage my time efficiently, deliver on time. I'm responsible and self-motivated. Some call me a high achiever.

Trouble is my performance reached a plateau a few years back and there's no hill in sight to climb.

I've been asking myself what I need to do to improve my results. I have no answer.

I gather top self-help books on how to be an effective leader, successful entrepreneur, innovative business owner. I scan them all, searching for the keys that might unlock the secrets to improving my performance. I feel hollow inside. Nothing resonates with my current experience. I stop reading.

I start to record myself in meetings (with permission). I listen to the recordings at night to observe my performance. I end up in tears at the things I miss in conversations and the mistakes I make. I stop recording.

And then I remember what it was like when I was learning to be a performer. I'd practice and practice and practice to get things perfect. And in between practicing, I'd work with coaches. These experts could hear my singing, see my dancing, observe my acting, and tell me where my strengths were, where I was still stuck, and where I could improve. They cared enough about my success to invent a way to pull me forward that would have me take the next step, and the next. And the hundred million steps after that.

It was always up to me to take each step. It was up to me to be responsible for my performance. Yet, each breakthrough performance was really courtesy of my coaches. Without them, I would never have known what hills I had to climb or how to get to the next level.

I want to move off this plateau. I want to succeed in the business world. I have a burning desire to be coached again.

And I'm ready.

MEETING JIM

As I prepare to talk with Coach Jim Hayford, I remember how committed my singing, speech, acting, and movement coaches were to helping me expand my capacity to be present, engaged, and ready to give my whole Being to every performance. I wonder if there are any common threads between the arts, sports, and business worlds in terms of coaching.

> Coach Jim Hayford is not someone you'd think would hire a coach to improve his performance. In 2011 he completed ten highly successful seasons as head basketball coach of Whitworth University's Pirates, a men's team he had built into an NCAA Division 3 powerhouse. Out of four hundred Division 3 schools, the Pirates had maintained the highest winning percentage in that entire time and closed the decade with a record of 217 wins to 57 losses (for a final percentage of 0.792). And when Coach Hayford left Whitworth to move to Eastern Washington University, he became one of only five coaches in the past decade to move directly from Division 3 to Division 1. Coach Hayford's record aside, he tells me it was his desire to improve his own performance as a coach that drew him towards working with an executive coach who had a solid background in athletics and rugby.

I wonder what an executive coach could contribute to someone who is already an "all-star" coach.

> Hayford, himself a former scholarship soccer player, wanted to keep seeing from the perspective of a coachee while he took on

coaching the EWU Eagles. He wanted to understand for himself what it would be like for the members of a team that hadn't had a winning season in five years to be coached by him—someone new coming in from a decade-long winning streak, someone who hadn't recruited them, someone who would be asking them to think critically about their own choices.

"The days of a coach doing all the talking and the players doing all the listening are over. When I was growing up, you would never question the coach. That's the way you did it. End of conversation. I think more so now, everything's up for debate."

Coach Jim Hayford, Head Coach,
Eastern Washington University's Eagles

So the call for transparency and accountability in corporate leadership has a parallel in athletics. An athletic coach's approach to leadership and communications can influence team performance just like the CEO's approach can shape organizational culture and performance.

Great coachees are often confident workaholics: they have an insatiable appetite for improving their performance, an aptitude for learning, and a desire to be successful. They welcome conversations that help them find ways to be the very best they can be. Hayford was no exception. He started working with his own coach a few months after arriving at EWU. Some of the strategies and techniques his coach initially suggested he chose to follow, others he chose not to based on his own experience. The process of considering each suggestion was valuable in itself, for it had Jim carefully look at why he was doing what he was doing and then assess whether it was the best way. Hayford appreciated his coach's graciousness and knew that the final decisions were always his own to make.

Since a university basketball coach spends more time per week and per semester with their team members than any other faculty member, they can have a profound influence and impact on the lives of their players. Coach and players are with each other—breathing, eating, sleeping, and developing basketball skills—seven months of the year full-time and five months of the year part-time. Throughout the year, the players have an opportunity to pick up values and experience from the college basketball curriculum that can help them be successful in any profession they choose to pursue. Values like accountability, personal responsibility, teamwork, discipline, effort, resilience in overcoming adversity, maturity.

Just like in business. Building a solid foundation for teamwork often starts with common values.

Coach Hayford took a page from his coach's book in the first year with the Eagles. He applied an inquisitiveness and gracious approach to his own coaching, only to discover that these college players were used to either doing what they were told—no questions asked—or subtly resisting instruction.

The opportunities for learning and development expand significantly when you engage people in exploring together what works best for them, what doesn't, and why. So rather than being manipulative and controlling, Hayford started having one-on-one dialogues with players around the question why whenever they demonstrated they were resisting his coaching—either through their words or their actions on the court. Sometimes they were unwilling to try a new technique because they didn't believe it was in their best interests. Sometimes they were having difficulty with implementation. Sometimes they were having trouble accepting a new way of doing things. Whatever the reason, together they explored each other's perspective and what was happening in the game to come up with something that could work for player, coach, and team.

This reminds me of the approach some directors take in working with singers and actors. Discover together what will work best for the individual performer, the director, the ensemble, and the production.

Some of my colleagues found this more collaborative style of directing difficult to get used to at first, but in the end, performances seemed to go much more smoothly when we had worked this way through all the rough spots in a production.

This new approach didn't result in immediate successes on the scoreboard for the Eagles. Five weeks into the season, Coach Hayford realized his own relationship to the losses was affecting his presence as a leader. He had to find another way to measure success rather than simply looking at the team's scores—a way that could better support their collective shift to a winning culture.

His coach showed him how to respond to what was happening in a way that kept the team's spirits high. Obviously, as competitors in a league, the Eagles couldn't lose sight of the scoreboard: what shows up there is the team's "bottom line" in terms of their standing in the league. However, they could start with acknowledging that the best teams in the country miss half their shots on basket and that an essential part of the game is about improving skills gradually so that fewer of your shots fail. Rather than looking *only* at the scoreboard, they began to celebrate their small victories within practices and games and to view those as preparations for future achievements. Whether those small victories were being a little stronger or understanding the game a bit better or using a specific technique with more ease, it didn't matter.

"I don't think it's important what you're teaching or what you're coaching. *It's about what they're learning and what they're doing.* In my coaching, I want them to know why they are doing what they are doing. It's not so important that they listen to me as much as they speak back to me with their own voice."

Coach Jim Hayford

Hayford also began working with his coach to improve his own efficiency as a leader by simplifying and optimizing the organization's processes and systems. The introduction of all these changes positively impacted the team and paved the way for Jim's biggest takeaway from his executive coach: mastering how to deal with moods.

Up until this time, Coach Hayford had simply relied on his innate ability in working with moods. He knew that the frame of mind of each player and the overall mood of the team impacts how each person plays and how well the team plays together. His coach equipped him to understand, diagnose, and rebuild mood, and guided him in incorporating these capacities into his own highly relational coaching style.

Improving your efficiency and increasing your ability to deal with moods: these could help almost any leader in any environment.

Now Coach Hayford frequently and regularly asks his players how he can coach them better. Their responses help him understand how to tailor his coaching to each of the team's fifteen individual basketball players and three assistant coaches and more accurately diagnose each person's mood, energy, and performance. He invests the time necessary to develop a solid foundation of trust and relationship with each assistant coach and each player. And he evaluates each person's mood—and the mood of the Eagles overall—on an ongoing basis.

The conversations Coach Hayford has with his players turn mistakes and failures into teachable moments. They often go further than the basketball court: he challenges them to succeed with their academic work, to be disciplined and to work hard, to be accountable to their team members and responsible for their choices and their performance on the court and in life. And he gets results.

Under first-year head coach Jim Hayford, the Eagles have experienced improvement—and success. They recently won six road games (the most since 2002 and an improvement of five games over last year) and experienced their first non-losing conference season. They made it into the Big Sky Conference Championship, where they advanced through the quarter finals before falling to Montana (74–66) in a game where they led 62–61 until the last two minutes. Their first player was honored on the All Big Sky Conference first team and the BSC All Tournament squad. And their fans have taken notice: game attendance doubled over last season and closed with the ninth and tenth highest single recorded attendances in EWU history for their semi-finals with Montana.

Coach Hayford obviously knows what it takes to build a championship team—and men who will become champions. I believe Eastern Washington University is fortunate to have hired a coach who has dedicated his life to getting better every day.

REFLECTING

My conversation with Coach Hayford impressed on me that the coaching relationship has the potential to show us our greatness and to help us achieve greatness. No matter what's at stake in the coaching—a relationship, a career, a team, a business—trust is the quintessential ingredient for success. **Without deep trust, no coaching can occur.**

> "The authentic coaching relationship is a bilateral trust-based agreement. As a coachee, you have to trust that I'm competent to produce on this transformation I'm promising. I have to trust that you are serious and willing to be rigorous and will grant me the authority to work with you. Every interaction we have is trafficking in this currency of trust. With a high level of trust, you can do all sorts of stuff because you're not caught up in posture and pretense. Absent that, nothing much will happen."
>
> Chris Majer

This is not the simple or blind trust of hope: it's trust based in a belief that you can get the job done together because of who you both are and what you each bring to the relationship. Both parties contribute to generating trust in several ways.

Great coaches maintain impeccable confidentiality. They set clear parameters for the coaching engagement and explicitly ask permission before sharing anything from their coaching sessions with anyone—including the identity of their clients. Many coaches I spoke with pointed out that coachees who work with "internal coaches"— managers or leaders charged with coaching others inside their own organization—often limit how far they will go in their coaching because of this. Their coach may inadvertently disclose something said in a coaching conversation to their boss. Or their coach may unconsciously put forward their own agenda in a coaching interaction, rather than remaining true to a commitment to the coaching relationship's objectives. On the other hand, "external" coaches—free agents or representatives from a firm outside the organization—will often discuss guidelines for the coaching up front with each coachee, aligning on the objectives of their work together and clarifying what will and what will not be shared with people's managers and the human resources department.

Great coaches don't hold back with their coachees. They model what it is to have authentic, sincere conversations without any hint of manipulation. They listen deeply and generously, and they speak from a place of acceptance and non-judgment. They hold their client's agenda as their own, and inspire credibility and confidence with their integrity in keeping that agenda front and center. They avoid becoming attached to any prescriptive analysis they may make about what a coachee needs; they stay focused on where each person is in the moment and what they're up for, while maintaining a clear connection with the client's commitments.

"My commitment is to help you achieve *your* commitments. We're not playing a game with each other. I trust that what you're saying to me is how you see it. Real straight talk. You're not consciously holding back, covering over, hiding, stepping over things. As a coach, I help you see where you might be doing that unconsciously. Seeing your own blind spots, is, by definition, impossible. We are blind to the fact that we are blind. So an important part of my value as a coach is to shine a light on your blind spots. I rarely give advice. I do help you see things that you don't see, that you don't even know that you don't see. And that makes a huge difference to the choices you have for action."

Don Arnoudse

Great coaches and their coachees fulfill their promises to each other. They have confidence in each other's competence, capabilities, and capacity to deliver on what they promise. And they call each other on unfulfilled promises.

"The coaching relationship is a set of conditional promises. If you fulfill on your promises and I fulfill on mine, the promise of the outcome and the result is pretty much assured. It's not necessarily because either of us are great. It's because the practices and the steps are trustworthy."

Jennifer Cohen

Great coaches take people where they have gone themselves. There is no substitute for direct personal experience. Coach Hayford's coach could observe and guide him based on his own training, experience, and grounding in transformation. His coach was not simply a subject matter expert who had added coaching skills to an already comprehensive tool kit. Instead of going for incremental change, Hayford was inspired and supported by his coach in going for whatever he thought was possible for himself and his basketball team. Coach Hayford's commitment to self-improvement in service of the Eagles brought forth his own transformation—as well as theirs.

Coaches often—but not always—have relevant expertise they can call on. Coach Hayford trusted his coach could understand the world of university basketball coaching based on his own background as a rugby player, aikido practitioner, and business leader. Although his coach may not have had all the language and rules of basketball at his fingertips, he could easily learn them—if necessary. Their work, however, didn't need to focus on things that Coach Hayford had long ago mastered.

The opportunity was really to draw on his coach's knowledge and wisdom to more effectively read his team, listen deeply to what was in the background, generate and enroll everyone in a compelling vision of the future, and create new stories about how they could live into that future individually and together. Over time, Hayford was also able to bring some of the distinctions of transformation to his leadership so he could more efficiently establish and maintain relationships based on trust, shift moods, and mobilize action.

"Coaching is about improving human performance, human presence, human capacity."

Mark Cappellino

Trust showed up as being absolutely essential to coaching in all the interviews I conducted. I especially found it intriguing that almost every coach I talked with trusts at least one other person to be their "coach" or their "committed observer." The trend seems to be for novice coaches to start out with one regular coach they rely on, intermediate coaches tend to have one or more, and master coaches have a network of coaches and trusted professional colleagues they call on for specific, laser-like coaching conversations. Several very experienced master coaches also shared that they live life being open to coaching from everyone and everything. For them, coaching is a way of relating to themselves and the world. Several senior coaches I spoke with said that, in their experience, coachees who demonstrate a strong desire and commitment to self-improvement, coupled with self-trust, humility, and vulnerability, often have the potential themselves to become great coaches.

INTEGRATING

When I was training as a performer, there were times when I would find myself working with several coaches at once. Sometimes with a team of coaches collaborating on a particular project or production. Sometimes with a variety of unrelated coaches working independent of each other on improving specific skills. Those I trusted most helped me improve the most.

So far, it seems that desire, commitment, and trust form the foundation of an effective coaching relationship. With these in place with a coach, I could perhaps let go of being attached to my hard-won proficiencies and open up to further learning and development.

Who knows what I might then discover about myself and in what ways I might grow?

A master in the art of living draws no sharp distinction between his work and his play, his labour and his leisure, his mind and his body, his education and his recreation. He hardly knows which is which. He simply pursues his vision of excellence through whatever he is doing and leaves others to determine whether he is working or playing. To himself he always seems to be doing both. Enough for him that he does it well.

Lawrence Pearsall Jacks[1]

LEARNING

I don't separate my work from my life. So when I say I want to succeed in the business world, I'm really saying I want to succeed in life.

Maybe I don't really need a coach. Perhaps a mentor might be the way to go. Someone who could tell me what worked for them. Someone to show me the ropes. Someone to teach me what the rules are for living successfully.

They say you don't get what you want, you get what you need.

Well, a master coach has appeared in my life.

Someone whose life is a work of art. Someone who is wisdom and compassion and courage. Someone whose presence inspires me to aspire to something greater, something I desire with all my being: a life of happiness, well-being, love, and fulfillment. A true master in the art of living.

I want to learn how to have my life be a work of art.

I've accepted without hesitation his offer to be my coach.

MEETING SUMANT

I can hear a student knocking at my neighbor's door as I start to call the senior VP and Chief Scientific Officer at Hospira, Inc., a global health-care pioneer in innovation and safety. My neighbor teaches English privately at her home, and every once in awhile, I see her young foreign students coming and going. As I listen to the phone ringing, I wonder whether my new coach will make an assessment about whether I'm coachable just as teachers might make assessments about whether their students are teachable. Or whether he'll limit his assessments to whether I'm "game-ready." The question will have to wait, as I focus on the voice coming across the line.

Sumant Ramachandra starts by telling me he believes that coaching is key in growing people, and that we learn before we grow. Before joining the world's leading provider of generic injectable drugs and integrated infusion technologies in 2008, he had focused his learning on three things: getting an MD and a PhD in medicine to become a physician-scientist, doing his internship and residency at Harvard Medical School–affiliated Massachusetts General Hospital to become a board-certified and licensed physician, and obtaining his MBA at Wharton to become an executive.

These learning successes were matched with a number of high-performing jobs in start-up, as well as established, endeavors. But after six months leading R&D at Hospira, Sumant received feedback that he was not effectively mobilizing people to deliver the value the company needed in terms of productivity, innovation, and sales. Seeing the need for an immediate turnaround, Sumant responded positively to then Chairman and CEO Chris Begley's request that he work with a coach.

"Sumant was coachable, smart, and receptive to feedback—all key criteria for a good coaching relationship. He loves to learn. He was getting feedback from many people—myself, the head of HR, the typical 360—looking for what he could do better and how he could improve. It almost became an overload. How could he prioritize all the different things he was being told? What are the common themes? What should he really focus on? Entered the coach."

Chris Begley, Former CEO & Chairman (retired), Hospira, Inc.

Sumant's sincere desire to be coached matched his commitment to the company's success. Uninterested in incremental changes for both the company and himself, he made a commitment to start with his own transformation. He chose a coach, someone known to the HR department, to work with him as a trusted advisor and as a catalyst to accelerate and realize his desire to become better.

I can certainly relate to wanting more than just incremental change. I wonder where Sumant and his coach focused first.

Together, Sumant and his coach reviewed the gap between his performance to date and the expectations of his boss and peers for an R&D transformation. He saw that his tendency to focus on speaking about individuals' strengths and positive qualities had unintended consequences: other people assumed he was blind to unresolved issues and the ways these were impacting the whole group.

"I may be well trained as a physician, a scientist, and a business person. But all of those skills are only a part of the foundation of what it takes to succeed as a senior executive. They are not the entire foundation."

Sumant Ramachandra, Senior VP and CSO, Hospira, Inc.

Sumant's speaking conveys the calm assurance of a leader who now knows what else it takes to succeed.

This senior VP learned that being more communicative and more collaborative could satisfy people's natural desire to know what he was noticing and doing. He immediately began sharing his intentions to address outstanding issues with his boss, his peers, and his direct reports in a way that respected their different perspectives and honored people's dignity.

Over the course of the next four months, he took on a significant workload, dramatically reorganizing his team and flattening the organization. He more than doubled the number of people reporting directly to him so as to be closer to the frontline staff. He began developing and promoting people internally, and he recruited new hires from diverse industries and different walks of life. This period marked the beginning of his learning journey.

"Every few weeks, I was pivoting to grow and grow and grow. At one point, my coach asked me why I talked about people, processes, and products...but never about driving for results. It was almost like an extra eye opened in my head. What stakeholders really care about is driving for results—and that you, your leadership, and your team will deliver these for the company."

Sumant Ramachandra

I'm reminded of Paolo and how coaching helped him deliver results in the midst of multiple crises. The more clear we can be up front in defining our intended outcomes, the more powerful a context we create for coaching. Within that context, a coach can firmly, compassionately, and nonjudgmentally confront any conflicts in our behavior, attitude, and values that stand in the way of progress.

With this new insight and his coach's guidance, Sumant reoriented himself to focus on creating a vision for the R&D

group, defining the shifts needed to realize that vision, and co-creating a strategy to manage the process. The strategic model he initially implemented achieved recognizable success and has since been adopted by other business units within Hospira.

When the company encountered a delivery challenge with two major products, Sumant was ready. He had developed his self-awareness and leadership capacity to the point where he could take breakdowns in stride, reorient himself in moments (rather than days), have open conversations without getting defensive, and create ways to get both programs back on track and approved by the FDA. As a leader to the teams involved and as point person to the Board of Directors, the federal regulatory agency, and investors, Sumant regularly communicated what was happening to all stakeholders in a transparent fashion and created an environment for success.

"When I hired Sumant, I knew he had only managed a handful of people. We threw him into a stretch position in a very complex R&D organization with close to a thousand people around the world. As much as one may love to learn, sometimes we need to have our behaviors and what needs to be changed explained to us. It's hard for a CEO to give that level of feedback on behavioral change when you're only exposed to each other in a handful of meetings. Sumant's coach was able to play that role for him. He grew tremendously. He went from being a facilitator to listening and then saying here's what we need to do. He developed a leadership style and the ability to know when to start generating the appropriate leadership direction. Coaching was extremely valuable for both him and the organization."

Chris Begley

Coaching isn't a head game. It's about applying our learning to the choices we have to make. The proof that learning has occurred shows up in our results.

> True success is measured by results over time. Since 2009 Hospira has measurably improved their new product process, funded several new innovation programs by reinvesting savings from organizational redesign, doubled the number of pharmaceutical development programs in its portfolio, and received approval for a major medical device. In 2010, at the conclusion of their coaching relationship, Sumant and his coach delivered a presentation to the Organization Development Network conference on how Hospira transformed their R&D organization.

> Today, Sumant is a trusted representative of the company, participating regularly as CSO with Hospira's CEO and CFO in their quarterly investor calls with Wall Street analysts.

This coaching relationship, like all the others I've seen so far, seems to have a natural life span that coincides with mastering what we need to learn and achieving our intended results. As I ring off from our call, I'm struck by how important listening is in all this.

REFLECTING

In effective coaching, the coach facilitates the coachee in their own unique learning process. There is no textbook one must follow. No predefined curriculum that must be delivered in a specific way.

> "For me, coaching is facilitating adaptive learning versus prescriptive action. A coaching relationship can almost always facilitate some shift in awareness. No matter what results you set out to achieve in a coaching conversation, there is always something to be learned."

> Mark Cappellino

Great coaches offer whatever they sense is needed in the moment in a person's life. Both individuals need to bring a special listening, a relaxed curiosity, and a humility to this work together.

Successful coachees listen for learning. Some people block learning opportunities when they come into coaching with an attitude of "I know that already!" or "I have better ideas than my coach." Others, addicted to novelty, discount anything they have heard before as having no value. Still others seek a magical silver bullet—a proven conceptual framework or model—on which to hang their expectations. Yet others love new insights, but have no real commitment to trying them out in action.

> "Sometimes we need evidence to see that we are causing the unwanted result or lack of high performance we could be getting. We cannot change something or address something we can't see: we cannot improve when we are blind to the reasons why we cannot improve. Real learning won't happen until we consider ourselves in need of coaching, when we have a genuine request. Until we declare ourselves incompetent, which simply means lacking competence (either totally or at some level) or that we want to get to another level, no learning, no progress can occur."
>
> Leslie Tucker, Roundstone International, Inc.

Coachees who are willing to listen from the perspective of "Who is my coach and what can I learn from them?" pull for the best from coaches. This way of listening—combined with commitment—can begin an iterative process of digesting ideas (without agreeing or disagreeing with them), testing them in action, assessing their effectiveness, making adaptations, and then testing again.

Coachees excel by listening to coaching as coaching—not as advice or answers. We can learn from advice, but we grow and evolve faster by making and acting on our own decisions. Coachees often find this confusing at first, since many coaches consult and many consultants coach.

Consulting focuses on identifying a "problem" and providing expert advice based on a perspective informed by experience and education. Anything that's heard as an expert opinion *and* a recommendation has the potential to block inquiry and learning and put the coach's agenda in front of the coachee's.

Great coaches distinguish between consulting and coaching early in the relationship and frequently point to it when they share their knowledge, experience, and perspective. In this way, they help their clients learn how to discern what is intended to be listened to as a recommendation versus a contribution towards broadening the client's own perspective or towards providing balance so a coachee can bring more traction, more thinking, or more kindness into what they're doing.

Coaches demonstrate profound listening. Profound listening transcends "active listening." Simply repeating back everything we've heard to make sure we've understood what's been said doesn't add significant value in a coaching interaction. Profound listening is about holding a person with "unconditional positive regard" and observing their essence and their deepest desires, their stated objectives and their hidden commitments, their self-awareness and their blind spots. It's about paying attention to their language, behaviors, and actions— what they avoid, what they get hung up on, what they repeat. And then responding to that individual in ways that facilitate their learning—including coaching, teaching, training, and mentoring—to develop awareness, skills, and competencies that help them grow in whatever ways they need to fulfill their commitments.

> "You have to be interested in what you're learning and hearing from your coachee—otherwise you can't bring an authentic level of inquiry and curiosity to the conversation."
>
> Dr. Carolyn Hendrickson, Tandem Group, Inc.

Great coaches discern "teachable moments." They accurately judge when their client is in a frame of mind conducive to learning, sense when they are ready to take in something that interrupts their habitual way of looking at or thinking about certain people or circumstances, know when a new distinction would be relevant. They read the other person *and* the coaching relationship at the same time and know whether both can hold what is arising. They have a knack for teaching—without knowing they're teaching. The interpretation that teaching is happening can only occur after the fact, when the coachee's results demonstrate they have learned and applied in their life what has been shared.

Coaches often develop this skillfulness over time, and are humbly aware, through experience, that they will not be able to coach everyone in every situation. Just as they are aware that not everyone who is willing and committed to being coached is necessarily open to coaching—or learning—in every moment. Sometimes the last thing people want to do is acknowledge that a distinction they've never heard before, a perspective they've never considered, or a possibility they've previously discarded is exactly what they need to look at to learn and grow.

INTEGRATING

I have no idea what I'll need to learn once I start working with my coach. What I'm looking to him for is a fresh perspective that might allow me to separate my aspirations and hopes from what's possible given who I am, what I'm willing to commit to, and my circumstances. Considering what's happening in my life right now, the time, energy, and resources required to manifest a particular dream may not be a price I'm willing to pay. Or it may be something I'm willing to change my entire life for.

In spite of all these unknowns going in, I'm looking forward to being coached. He's committed to developing people. Our initial conversation was unlike any I've ever had before. My coach speaks with compassion and wisdom of things I have never considered with anyone.

I feel as if he's really seeing me. As if he's looking through me and beyond who I present myself to be. I'm eager to learn from him. To look with him, through his eyes, at myself and the world. And then think for myself, choose what to do from there.

School never offered this kind of learning.

I'm looking forward to our shared journey.

My only concern: what if I undertake this journey and fail?

"One way to look at it is that there are two possibilities: it can be either a success or a learning experience."

Dr. Rick Fullerton, Fullerton Consulting

"We are players in a story where the clients are the stars. We show up infrequently, briefly, and only in supporting roles. The real drama is not about us, but about them."

Allan Henderson

DESIGN

Create the fantastic space. In performing arts lingo, that's how we referred to setting the stage for the magic of a live performance.

As performers, we knew it was up to us to create that magic.

When we succeeded, there was a palpable sense of connection with the audience. A sense of being fully present with each other. We'd arrive at the end of our time together, moved and inspired by what had happened in the space between us. When we failed, we all went back to our daily lives untouched.

We knew our success depended on generating a safe space—an oasis for Being—in which people would feel welcome and comfortable enough to join us in a shared journey.

Coaching sessions, like live theater performances, happen in a designed fantastic space. The only difference: coaching is not for public consumption. It's up to the coach and coachee—together—to create a private crucible for exploration, learning, and development.

Fantastic space is the safe harbor we co-create, the conversational space where we can begin the work of coaching.

> Your vision will become clear only when you look into your heart. Who looks outside, dreams. Who looks inside, awakens.
>
> Carl Jung[1]

ASSUMPTIONS & EXPECTATIONS

I'm hesitant and anxious and excited to start working with my coach.

At the most basic level, I'm hiring him to realize my full potential. At a much deeper level, I'm looking to my coach to help me go beyond who I *think* I am to discover who I *really* am. There's also the matter of exactly what I want to do and have in the second half of my life.

I always seem to bring hidden assumptions and expectations to any new relationship—even when I plan to come in with a blank slate. However much I try, I can't seem to shake the idea that my coach is going to change my life for the better. Everything that doesn't work now will work after coaching.

I'm expecting he will be able to help me question my own dogma about what the rules are for living successfully. I'm assuming he'll be able to see the mistakes I'm making and help me learn from them. I'm assuming he'll be able to help me overcome my weaknesses and show me what I need to give up to be successful. In my moments of weakness, I'm counting on him to point out where I'm not doing my best and to hold my feet to the fire when I drop back into procrastination or self-pity.

His calm confidence and professional credibility reinforce my belief that I can count on him to be in my corner—even when I give up on myself.

I wonder what his expectations are of me.

MEETING DAVID

I'm beginning to wonder if synchronicities are remarkable or ordinary. After all, it's me who declares something is synchronistic. It's me who finds a link between two disparate, seemingly unconnected events and makes meaning of that connection. Like the synchronicity I'm seeing in speaking with David Weaver just as I'm beginning to inquire into my own beliefs.

David is serious about questioning his own dogma. When he began working with a coach, he was looking for two things. His first expectation was for an objective perspective: he wanted someone who had no vested interest in the outcome of his choices, no preconceived notions about his history or what he had done, and no hesitation in challenging his basic assumptions. His second expectation: unadulterated honesty coupled with the courage to call him on any inconsistencies or bullshit observed in how he was living his life. David's relationship with his coach has turned out to be an ongoing process of self-discovery and creativity.

"Bringing creativity in is pure joy. Being in a meeting when that conversation starts—being present at that moment when the creative spark transpires—that's the human point. That's the transcendent moment that's interesting to me."

David Weaver, Independent Consultant

As a man raised in the American Midwest, David questioned the value of a coaching relationship. When he received the gift of a complimentary coaching session with a world-class coach, he resisted talking to her and decided to hand over the session to someone else. Believing that men don't have coaches, that as an adult you already have all the tools you need to succeed, and that only in-person meetings can guarantee results, he hesitated to call her, citing that she wasn't local and he didn't need coaching.

However, a few months later, when he acknowledged he was heading into a period of change, he realized he could perhaps benefit from working with her. Their initial conversations revealed his coach had a presence that transcended distance and technology and the key to realizing his fullest self-expression would come from his commitment to be in a coaching conversation, to do the work between sessions, and to get into the process and stay with it.

Interesting. I've heard from some people that they prefer coaching over the phone or on Skype because it forces them to be present and to turn off the things that would normally distract them.

Growing up, David had set his sights on becoming a lawyer, but when he entered college in 1984 he quickly realized that he was naturally drawn to marketing and advertising instead. For more than twenty years, David conceived and implemented strategies for some of the most respected and innovative companies in the world while working in and around ad agencies. This first iteration of himself (which he fondly called David 1.0) culminated in running a sixty-person ad agency with offices in New York and Dallas. Yet, in spite of having ticked off many of the boxes about what his life was supposed to look like, he wasn't totally happy. It was at this point that he began thinking of a change.

David soon found out that he couldn't lie to his coach: she had an uncanny ability to know when he wasn't speaking the truth— even if he didn't. Rather than let him run on autopilot, she would stop him and ask if he really meant what he said.

Interesting how we get what we ask for. David wanted a coach who wouldn't let him get away with any pretense. I want a coach who'll share unconventional wisdom and compassionately help me grow.

David also discovered that he couldn't phone in his sessions: he had to unplug from other distractions and be fully present in every coaching conversation. In doing so, he began to reconnect to his own voice.

"I think it's getting harder and harder to hear our own voices. It's easy to drown yourself out: just look at how few people on the subway don't have headphones in. There's something to be said for being in the same conversation, listening to each other, undistracted. When my coach is listening to me, it's easier to listen to myself. I find myself saying something and I go, 'Wait a minute, what did I just say and how does that connect?'"

David Weaver

David's coach invited him to look at where he was coasting, living in the future, or really being present to what he was feeling and wanting to create. Something in their early conversations prompted him to start the "RID Project," a creative self-experiment in letting go of the things he didn't care about to discover the things he did. David looked to his coach to help him identify practical steps that would help him realize this new vision of his self-expression.

They designed a disciplined way for him to give away possessions that were cluttering up his space—a way that would give him time to acknowledge what, if anything, each item meant to him as he let it go. He committed to let go of one thing per day for 365 days and to blog about his experience at www.whatigotridoftoday.com.

Before the end of the project, he gave away around 800 items and posted over 400 entries. The process of doing what many people talk about (but few do) and then sharing his experience of what he gained as he rid himself of belongings generated widespread interest. He was invited to speak at TEDxSMU in 2010, and then at TEDActive, TEDxPhoenix, and TEDxOmaha in 2011.

The only times I've consciously gone through my possessions is when circumstances have forced me to, like when I've had to move or clean up after a robbery or flood. It's felt freeing—and sometimes healing—to look at what I have and to let go of what I no longer need or want with me.

Running this project in tandem with his business tested more of David's assumptions about the world. He had assumed that people could only love one thing: if they liked one kind of music, they couldn't like another. If one person succeeded in business, that meant another was inherently failing. If David was doing poorly, then someone else was doing well. This perspective had him creating either/or solutions to problems and assessing every situation in terms of wins and losses. His coach helped him see that not only did this perspective add an unnecessary element of competition to all his relationships, but it also limited his creativity to two extremes.

"True creativity comes from restraint. Creativity is not about creating something beautiful and artistic without any parameters. A creative solution doesn't inherently reject constraints, but finds a way to embrace them and generate something that is original and inspiring. A thousand points exist between Points A and B. Discovering the thousand possibilities in between is actually true creativity."

David Weaver

This new perspective gave David the freedom to apply creativity to his own life in ways he never would have on his own. He recognized that music plays an important role in his happiness, which ultimately impacts how he engages with and reacts to the world. So he created more time in his life to enjoy the live performances that he loves.

Music used to contribute to my happiness. Perhaps that's why my coach has asked me why I'm not singing anymore.

Rather than thinking there is always only one winner in a situation, David stopped being overly concerned with his clients "winning" against their competition and began focusing more on developing strategies around what they do really well. And when he had taken a creative strategy as far as he could, David would let a colleague pick up the ideas and run with them. David's competitive approach was replaced with a more relaxed, collaborative stance and the joy of someone else adding to his strategic ideas to generate amazing things he couldn't even imagine.

Bringing a calm, mindful presence to work also now allows David to delve into the emotional side of customer interactions—so he can look at what really engages customers to want to buy from his clients and what has their customers run away. Using that deep understanding of customers and his own growing emotional awareness to develop strategies, David is helping his clients succeed on their own terms, irrespective of what their competitors are doing.

"All good creativity tends to come from our emotional side. That doesn't mean we don't have a good rational reason to do what we do. We've got to ask those basic questions *and* let our emotions rage a little bit to take it to something human and interesting."

David Weaver

Now I know why I've avoided music. It brings me in direct touch with my sadness around not having a career as a performer, my belief that I failed in the artistic game. And so I sought to escape into the business world. David's next words reveal another illusion I had—an illusion about business.

Looking at emotions in the context of business often seems out of place or counterintuitive for many Americans. Yet David tells me that as he works with his coach to develop the ability to be present with both the intellectual and the emotional aspects at play in any conversation, he finds himself becoming more trusting of himself and more even-keeled. Rather than being plagued with worries about what might happen, he can deal with setbacks more calmly and courageously. He can stay with what is, be committed to the process, and trust the outcome. His whole life is an expression of who he is becoming.

"For me, one of the strongest benefits of good coaching is I don't worry as much as I used to. That's not to say I don't have worries. But I just look at my life: I was born in a small farming town in Iowa, I graduated with twenty-seven people, and now I'm running an agency in New York. I instinctively made a bunch of good decisions. If I really think about that story that simply, it could scare me to death. The difference is that after spending time with my coach, I trust that's going to continue."

David Weaver

David is now exploring what the space he created with the RID Project is for. Whatever his next destination will be, he knows that his next steps will help him find out if that destination is really where he wants to go, or if another, better direction calls him.

Bringing a sense of exploration to coaching can help us see our own perspective and discover any thinking that limits us. As I hang up, I'm inspired by how clear David was about his expectations of his coach, how rigorously he has examined his dogma, and how fearlessly creative he is with his life.

REFLECTING

Due diligence pays. Checking into each other's background, sensing if you connect, clarifying the game: these begin the process of setting the stage. However, we also need to take our assumptions and expectations into account when designing a coaching relationship—just as we would if we were taking on a new job. Discussing the hidden assumptions we have about what we're up to and what we expect from each other creates a strong foundation for our work together.

> "Unmet expectations lead to upsets."
>
> Dr. Marc Cooper, The Mastery Company

Effective coaches surface expectations and assumptions early on. I discovered that many coaches often clarify what coaching will *not* be about in their first conversation with a prospective client. For example, a coach may declare they won't be:

- Giving you "the answers" to your "problems"
- Making your choices for you
- Supporting you (as in, holding you up or carrying you)
- Letting you get away with excuses
- Agreeing with your inner critic
- Judging you
- Relating to you as if you are "wrong"
- Shutting you down
- Manipulating you
- Managing you.

They may also speak to a coachee's silent expectation that, since they've been able to act as a genuine ally in helping others succeed, they will be able to help everyone succeed. While they may have the professional competence and experience to theoretically do so, their approach, style, background, and personality may not be the best fit for everyone's needs. Some coaches deal with this by offering an initial short-term engagement as a discovery period. Others have prospective clients complete online assessments and an intake interview with their staff. Still others listen for this fit in an initial consultation before committing to work with a new client.

A coach's initial assessment—whether it involves a rigorous intake process or is part of a more casual exploratory conversation—usually, but doesn't always, reveals whether coaching or therapy would best meet the individual's current needs. Unresolved issues from the past that require the help of a therapist and that may stand in the way of coaching or the client's well-being and success can be hidden from view at the outset, only to be revealed later while working together. It is up to the coach to bring their awareness of a need for therapy or help from other third parties to the individual's attention when they become aware of it.

Most great coaches work with clients they genuinely connect with and who are, at the very least, a request for coaching. In discovery, they listen for resonance with their own core values, knowing that any dissonance they have with what the person wants to work on, what they're concerned about in their current circumstances, or what they're committed to and most care about will only be amplified later on.

> "It's important to have some passion or interest about who they are, what they do, their style of thinking, and their willingness to have a beginner's mind and explore beyond their usual landscape. I am curious to see and understand the reason why people are doing the work they're doing in the world, if they are taking care of what they most care about, and if they are doing so in a big impacting way."
>
> Renee Freedman, The Freedman Collaboration Group

Some coaches also look for characteristics they believe to be critical for effective coaching to occur.

"When I meet a possible client, I ask my intuition, 'Is this a kindred spirit? Do they think? Is this person up to what I'm up to on the planet? Are they willing to do anything? Do they have a track record of taking risks and taking care of people? Do they have some transformational intent? Are they values-based, and are they competent?' Those are the individuals whom I can commit myself to."

Charles E. Smith, Kairos Productions Inc.

Coaches listen for desire, knowing that the level of a person's commitment to receiving coaching influences what's possible. Someone who doesn't even pretend to listen to coaching will get nothing from a coaching interaction. Someone who listens to coaching selectively will only get what they choose to get. Clients who listen to coaching anytime will get slightly more value than those who are a request for coaching. Those who demand effective coaching will get the most value of all.

Coachees who benefit the most from coaching expect greatness from themselves *and* their coaches. Coachees, although they don't have as much experience to draw on in assessing whether a coach is the right fit for them, would be wise to do so. It's worth examining any assumptions you may have that a specific coach is committed to your commitments, that they will respect confidentiality in the ways you want, and that they will be competent in enabling you to achieve the results you want.

Relevant life experience and values that align with or complement your own may be necessary, along with the fundamental ability to observe your thinking process. Coaches need to be able to get inside your thinking, ask questions that others won't, and inspire confidence to go beyond what *feels* reasonable and safe. The way you think— whether linear or nonlinear—and the boundaries you want set around confidentiality don't tell them who you are. But they do reveal how you're likely to express yourself and how you'll relate to taking care of what you care about. When you move beyond the initial getting acquainted stage, that awareness can help them effectively say what they see and do what needs to be done—regardless of its potential cost to them—and invoke the same honesty and committed action in you.

> "There's a point where I move from just listening, trying to gather information and make sense, to where it's all integrated, and I can ask provocative questions that open awareness and introspection into how they are thinking or assessing the world and their place in it. I love to integrate everything so that the way people live their life, do their work, and serve their purpose reflects what they're passionate about. To bring things out so that how they move with what they care most about is how they lead and move through life. So that their passion invites others in."
>
> Renee Freedman

Effective coaches set clear boundaries and create the context of the coaching relationship. While it is up to both coachee and coach to design the ground rules of working together (when, where, and how often they will meet, what the engagement will involve, how information will be handled), it is the coach who creates the confidential container in which the alchemical work of coaching will occur. Great things can emerge from the intimate crucible of an extraordinary coaching relationship. Seasoned coaches know the experience of being cared about and profoundly "heard" and "seen" by another person—without being judged—can easily be mistaken for something else.

Being clear about boundaries that honor and empower both people up front allows for coachee and coach to bring their full selves to the work. To that end, professional coaching organizations, such as the International Coach Federation (ICF), have established codes of conduct and ethical standards requiring coaches to set clear, appropriate, and culturally sensitive boundaries around confidentiality, care, and physical contact with clients.

> "The relationship is intimate because people are telling you things they've, in some cases, never said to anyone. As they get more and more comfortable, they just launch into 'open the kimono' mode. There's a whole confusion about what feelings we are having here and why. There's a reason the ICF has a rule against dating or having any kind of relations with your coachee, and that's because it can get there very easily."

> Michael McDermott, Arcadia Group

For employees involved in formal in-house coaching programs, being honest about the boundaries of the relationship from the start can help minimize train wrecks down the line. If both parties to an in-house coaching relationship agree that their coaching interactions will remain within the realm of mentoring about professional development and advising about work-related matters, then both will know what is and what is not safe to bring into the context of their coaching conversations.

> "I am a conduit for people to reach into their highest and best self and take a stand. To truly be coached is to bring your full self into the relationship. And to do that one needs to feel comfortable and safe. Rarely is it possible for people to be able to relate in that way to their direct manager or second-in-line. Some informal mentoring relationships can resemble coaching if the mentor is very, very skilled. However, in my observation, many mentors don't have the distinctions, the boundaries, or the rigor that are necessary in a coaching relationship."

> Gina LaRoche, Seven Stones Leadership Group LLC

Confidentiality assurances aside, internal coaches are human beings: they cannot "unhear" what they have heard. Whatever you share in a coaching conversation with a coworker or boss has the potential to impact how they listen to and perceive you in the future—both of which can influence your career.

Great coaches generate coaching as an inquiry. Effective coaches listen to learn in every moment. They're curious to know our assumptions and expectations, our mindset and beliefs, our commitments and concerns, our purpose and passions, our circumstances and challenges, as well as how we're relating to whatever is happening in our life. Coaches take in both the verbal and the nonverbal, the conscious and unconscious. They use all senses to observe the entire person. They take in information from many different sources, including: body, mood, tone of voice, nuances of language, range of emotion, pace, energy, and focus. They pay attention to all the systems at play in the coachee's world—from the person's physiology to the networks of relationships they operate in and their connectedness with their environment. They also read what's happening in the fantastic space, in the silences and in the things not said in a coaching relationship itself.

> "Coaching is an exploration to help folks expand, shift, change how they see, evaluate, and interpret the world and themselves. We as coaches open up a broad spectrum of ways to see and move in the world: that allows them to consider things in a much more whole fashion. It allows them to bring a different observer, to take different actions and have different conversations. We end up transforming our clients in some way through coaching."
>
> Renee Freedman

As David saw, this deep, confidential exploration can happen virtually via phone or video phone. Great coaches are great "bullshit detectors." They can sense incongruity, inauthenticity, and misalignment and effectively push into what is blocking us from accomplishing our goals.

That's why we hire them.

INTEGRATING

I want to be related to in this profoundly rigorous way. And so I've made my demand for effective coaching clear to my coach. We've agreed on matters of confidentiality, logistics, and ethics.

After context-setting comes content.

I wonder what we'll discover in our exploration.

> "Until you identify yourself as incompetent and declare you want to get to another level, there's no learning. Learning doesn't happen until you consider yourself a beginner."
>
> Leslie Tucker

COMPETENCY

I've made it halfway through life. And I still desire to become more competent, more confident, more capable of contributing to others.

I am clear with my coach today that I'm not interested in incremental improvements or a quick fix. I want long-lasting results. I want to ditch anything that's keeping me stuck and keep whatever I need to move forward.

To be honest, I've got no idea what that will take. That's why I tell him I'm relying on *his* competence as a coach to help me figure out what I should be doing at this point in my life.

His response floors me.

He says coaching is not a magic bullet and he's not here to fix me...because there's nothing wrong with me. He doesn't have the answers. And he won't be making choices for me.

He says he will help me engage with the tough questions I need to ask myself. We'll be in this inquiry together. In the spirit of a shared adventure, we can discover what's missing for me to be fulfilled, happy, and satisfied and, from there, look at what I may need to learn, what competencies I may need to develop, what resources I may need to generate.

I hadn't really anticipated taking time out now to look at where I'm heading, why I'm doing what I'm doing, and whether I've got the relationships, the skills, and the tools I need to be successful. Yet, if I'm going to move beyond standstill, now is the time to dive deep into these questions. Looks like we're going to be exploring unknown territory together.

I'm glad I have a partner in this inquiry.

MEETING MS. FORST

When I was studying music, I didn't consider all the competencies one would need to be a performing artist. In my youthful enthusiasm, I didn't know enough to discern what's needed to be successful in the business of opera. Today I have the privilege of being able to finally close that gap by speaking with a master opera singer, Canadian mezzo-soprano Judith Forst.

Ms. Forst delights audiences around the world with her performances. Known as "one of the few truly world-class coloratura mezzo-sopranos on the operatic stage,"[1] she has enjoyed a thriving international career for more than four decades. Starting with her debut at the Met at the age of twenty-four, she has performed extensively in major opera houses throughout North America and Europe for over three decades. In 1991 she was made an Officer of the Order of Canada. Ten years later, she was awarded the Order of British Columbia. Today, aspiring opera students look to Ms. Forst as a teacher, mentor, and model of success. Many are surprised to learn that, even with all her knowledge and professional experience, she continues to work with multiple coaches to learn new roles and to prepare roles she has done many times in the past.

Our conversation begins with a similar kind of focus and impeccability.

Ms. Forst starts by telling me that opera is not just beautiful music: it is hard work.

"Music is a business. You have to treat it like one. It's not just about buying the pretty dress for the audition. You can wear the pretty dress, but if you haven't got the goods or the instrument, the style, the correctness, you're not going to get the part."

Judith Forst, OC, OBC

Coaching is an integral part of the professional opera singer's life. Throughout their training and careers, singers look to coaches to help them develop skills and abilities and to prepare to perform. Young opera students can call on their coaches to help them develop competencies in style, musicality (pitch, rhythm, harmony), intonation, languages, diction, and characterization. While they develop all these aspects of performing with a coach, they also need to learn how to work with their body, their energy, and their moods in their singing. Talent scouts and opera houses can quickly distinguish between a performer who is bringing their whole self to their singing and someone who is not fully present and engaged.

As I listen to Ms. Forst speak of what's needed to begin a professional career in this field, I can now see how I fell short in some essential areas of competence and did passably well in others. My failure to launch a successful singing career could be partly attributed to the inaccurate self-perceptions of competence I had in my youth. As this successful performer continues to speak, I'm reminded that more is needed than just competence.

Coaches also help singers at any stage of their career with developing and finessing their repertoire. There is a constant need to have a variety of pieces and roles ready when audition opportunities arise. Once contracted, singers are expected to come to rehearsal with the words, music, and basic characterization of their role mastered. Once in production, they work with the coaches the opera company has on staff while they learn and integrate the director's staging into their performance. These staff coaches can also help pinpoint and address small issues that may creep into a singer's performance during the run of a production before they become problems.

Some singers, once they are well-established in their careers, choose to stop working with coaches outside of the production period. Others, like Ms. Forst, prefer to continue to invest in coaching to ensure they can evolve their repertoire as they grow older and continue to deliver their best in each and every performance.

I remember how much I disliked the process of learning new songs, and how much I loved stepping into the characters and learning their words and their way of thinking. Exploring the subtleties of acting and language interested me much more than distinguishing between the different "colors" of a sung vowel. My current commitment to clarity and effectiveness with words is like Ms. Forst's obvious passion and dedication to thorough preparation for performing opera.

Ms. Forst chooses to work with coaches she either knows personally, has observed in action, or has been referred to by a trusted colleague. Like any successful business person, she expects a certain level of professionalism and credibility from her coaches. They must have credentials and a clear intention and commitment to her, they must give her their undivided attention during their time together, and they must communicate their ideas to her in ways that she can use.

"Other people know things you need to know. I always need the ears of the coach. You can only do so much from a book. You need somebody to guide you through the dos and don'ts, the pitfalls, the way to get the sound true. You need somebody who is concentrating as hard as you are."

Judith Forst

After Ms. Forst does the groundbreaking work of learning the notes of a new role alone, she calls on specific individuals from her network of coaches to help prepare for the production. Although she plays the piano herself, she will take the opera to a coach to work through and practice difficult sections—sometimes going from the beginning to the end of the piece as if she were performing the entire role. If the opera is in a foreign language like Russian or Czech, she will work with a coach specializing in that particular language to master the intricacies of pronunciation and diction. Depending on the piece she'll be performing, she may also travel to New York to work with a senior coach who specializes in that particular musical genre to finesse stylistic nuances and ensure she is on top of the latest performance trends in that field.

I'm beginning to sense a drive and intensity towards mastery here that reminds me of Sumant's commitment to ongoing learning.

These senior coaches, highly valued and highly paid, tend to work in the major opera houses. By working constantly with the best conductors in the world, they become familiar with the "five possible ways" a phrase can be sung. All ways are valid, and a conductor can call on a singer to use any of the ways at any time. The final authority in any production, of course, is the conductor—who is also the singer's coach. For Ms. Forst, knowing what those five ways are well before she goes into rehearsal is invaluable. It allows her the time to practice and become competent enough with the different approaches to know what is possible when it comes time to deliver whatever the conductor asks for.

I see mastery is not about knowing it all. Mastery is about developing expedient, skillful means.

Pulling together the input she has received from all of her coaches, Ms. Forst is fully prepared to work when she arrives at the first day of rehearsal. And with her extensive industry experience, she has the credibility and confidence to masterfully work with conductors and directors as colleagues in rethinking trouble spots during the rehearsal process.

"We're here to work."

Judith Forst

For opera singers, this ability to pull together multiple coaching perspectives is key. If they can stay open to looking at new possibilities, be self-aware as they try out anything new, and then process all that information, they can figure out what works best for them from the different levels of coaching they have received.

This mirrors the approach of master coaches I've spoken with calling on trusted professional colleagues for specific coaching.

Ms. Forst finds that young singers often look to their coaches and teachers for the magic bullet. She encourages those who aspire to become professional singers to work with different coaches and teachers, but to find their own magic bullet.

It is the singer's responsibility to know their body and their voice and what feels comfortable in their throat. It is their responsibility to know themselves well enough to be able to discern when they are just afraid of doing what's been asked of them and when that request will really put them in trouble if they do it. It is their responsibility to manage their energy well enough to reach the end of each performance—night after night.

At the end of the day, Ms. Forst knows it is her reputation—not that of her coaches—that is on the line every time she goes on stage. It's up to her to deliver results.

I now see that Ms. Forst's capacity to generate extraordinary performances year after year is based in solid competencies, a keen business sense, and never-ending practice and study. She knows where she excels, what repertoire works best for her voice, age, and presence. She picks the right projects. She has the capacity to balance the physical, dramatic, and vocal demands of each production with the director's staging and the conductor's musical choices. Her discipline, persistence, and commitment to coaching continue to pay off. She works with coaches she trusts. And she continues to evolve as a singer, an artist, and a human being.

REFLECTING

Above and beyond having the requisite talent, knowledge, skills, and attributes expected in their chosen field, successful professionals like Ms. Forst often demonstrate an unshakable commitment to doing the work. They will often look for a coach who is effective—if not masterful—at developing people's potential. They need to be able to trust their coach to help them *see* and *hear* themselves more accurately and completely.

> "Coaching is about creating a new observer. You can't act on what you can't see. When the coachee stands in the perspective that 'I can't see the back of my own head,' new vistas are possible. Coaching is a way for people to see what they may not observe in the moment—then blind spots, robotic behavior, and unconscious patterns can be revealed and new choices can be made."
>
> Vince DiBianca, Praemia Group LLC

In that respect, the coach's competency and credibility influence what's possible in their work with a coachee. Unfortunately, much consumer confusion exists around the whole topic of coach competencies and credibility.

Coaching is a nebulous service, not easily explained to those who haven't experienced it. As an emerging field, a general consensus on certification and educational standards has not yet been reached. Many "master" coaches in the field today are not certified at all: they have been working as coaches since before coaching was a recognized profession. To get established in this industry, younger generations of coaches often complete a certain number of hours of classroom training, mentoring, and practical experience to meet certification standards. However, unlike fields that involve postgraduate education at a college or university, coach training doesn't have entrance requirements. Without an initial "screening" process in place, people may graduate still lacking fundamental attributes and competencies essential for "being" a coach. Many people rely on word of mouth, referrals, or verifiable testimonials to find effective coaches with credibility and integrity.

> "Coaching is a relationship. It's a conversation you are involved in with someone else about them. For the relationship to really be valuable and ongoing and lasting, the coach has to be competent in dancing in whatever that relationship is and be effective and have the person grow."
>
> Marcia Martin, MM Productions

There appear to be several competencies essential for effective coaching in addition to what I've discovered so far.

Great coaches bring a powerful presence to their work. They demonstrate an ability to be focused, flexible, open, and present. They trust and act on their intuition. They can be with strong emotions and conflict. They say they don't know when they don't know. And they bring humor and lightness into conversations about serious matters.

Effective coaches can design ways to close the gap between where their clients are now and where they need to be to succeed. That means they know their own strengths and capabilities, and can make accurate assessments about other people's competencies and needs.

A coach who works with someone they know can't benefit from coaching—either because they're not the right "fit" or because this isn't the best approach for this individual at this time—lacks integrity.

Similarly, a coach who cannot discern when they don't have sufficient competency to work with an individual jeopardizes the success of both parties. For example, if your capabilities as a novice opera coach encompass only the mechanics of notes, rhythms, and harmonies, being in integrity could include referring a young singer to a singing teacher when they are experiencing problems with their vocal technique, rather than risking that artist's voice (and possibly career) with your primitive instructions.

Similarly, a coach who withholds valuable learning or who cannot meet people where they are cannot call forth their client's greatness. A coach who excels at making business skills and concepts artist friendly but holds back this key aspect of entrepreneurialism from talented visual artists would do them a disservice. Very few of the coaches I interviewed rely on a preset curriculum for their one-on-one coaching. Instead, they focus on engaging with the coachee in the moment and creating what's needed from there.

Competent coaches help us embrace our own incompetence.
Coaching doesn't always focus on developing strengths. Sometimes it's necessary to become competent in areas that don't come naturally to us. Competent coaches help us give up any story we may have about not being good enough or talented enough, and get on with the work of developing ourselves.

"Taking a person's talents and skills and helping develop them as big as you can and then connecting that to the soul: that's the 'greatness' coaches look to call forth in people."

David Boothroyd, University of British Columbia
Opera Ensemble

Creative entrepreneurs, for example, often find the business planning process challenging because it's not normally approached in a visual, free-form way. When these people find a coach who can translate the traditionally linear, structured way of thinking about planning into something they can access, they can start to develop competency in this area. Visual artists face a similar challenge.

"Visual artists tend to have difficulty with detailed, step-by-step linear thinking. I don't do it for them. I show them how to do it for themselves. I ask the questions that help artists discover their skill and how to use their own creativity in building a career. They are the ones who make things happen. Coaching becomes a dramatic kind of learning and confidence-building for artists."

Dr. Mary Edwards, Coaching for Artists &
Creative Entrepreneurs

Effective coaches have a proven framework of distinctions behind their thinking. They don't teach people ideas or a specific methodology simply for the sake of sharing teaching. They share distinctions relevant to the work at hand—distinctions they embody themselves—in a way that coachees can experience them fully and then apply in their lives. Great coaches also have the capacity to help their clients master distinctions so they can generate them on their own, rather than having to rely on their coach forever.

Using distinctions as tools of interpretation, coachees may find themselves suddenly able to distinguish subtle changes in the timbre of a vowel they've just sung, the effect of various postures or facial expressions on their energy level, the impact of a new interpretation of profit and loss statements on their team's mood, or the consequences of an unresolved conflict on their performance at work. Learning distinctions in this way can help expand a person's capacity to observe themselves, their perceptions and point of view, their interpretations and assessments, their abilities and obstacles. All this can help people break through resistance and get into action.

Competent coaches share multiple ways of looking at and doing things. Being coached isn't about learning "the right way" to do something. It's about becoming competent in the *ways* that can work for you. That's why singers, for example, can study with multiple coaches simultaneously. Each coach brings their unique set of distinctions to the work: what one hears or sees, another may be totally blind to. What one coach eagerly dives into, another may not even cover. It's up to the coachee to take the best of what each coach offers and make it their own.

> "Much in the field of opera is subjective. There are many ways of doing something 'right.' I recognize that other coaches and conductors will have other ideas about what doing it 'right' looks like. I point out to young singers that, ultimately, the only person who is 'right' is the one who is paying you at the moment."
>
> David Boothroyd

Great coaches use the tools of listening and speaking to operate with laser-like precision. Great coaches adapt their listening, verbal style, and pace to suit the moment-by-moment needs of each client. They continuously strive to find a way to connect with their coachees so their clients don't have to be any different than they are. The more comfortable people feel about expressing the full range of their emotions in their coach's presence (their anger, sadness, disappointment, and frustration), the more likely they will relax and feel they can go anywhere in their coaching.

> "Communication skills is being with a person in a way that you're connected, sharing an experience with that person, being able to speak in a way that's inspirational and sensitive and that opens up possibilities and allows a person to get closer to something they hadn't noticed before."
>
> Marcia Martin

When a coach speaks, they also simultaneously listen for the impact of their speaking. They focus on the client and watch to see what message is being received, and then course-correct for any unclear meanings or misunderstandings that arise from the limitations, nuances, or standard interpretations of a particular language or culture. At the end of the day, it's more important that the coachee understand what's being shared than that the coach sound intelligent or look good.

> "It has been a wonderful learning for me to keep getting pushed back into meaning, rather than being restricted to what language makes easily available. For example, lots of vocabulary was lost during the Cambodian Genocide, so the interpreters there had to reintroduce words and constructs that people were no longer using in order to get our points across accurately. Similarly, when I was working in Nepal, my team ended up going back to Sanskrit to find language to convey our meaning."
>
> Allan Henderson, GHJ Consulting

Unlike a friend or spouse, an effective coach will ask you powerful questions that can make you uncomfortable and they may say things you would rather not hear. They will call on a variable mix of relevant metaphors and personal stories, potent challenges, skillful interjections, sensitive jokes, and silence. Focused, direct communications like these can open the doorway to big breakthroughs, especially if you have nowhere else in your life to have these conversations.

INTEGRATING

My coach certainly has made me uncomfortable already. But it's a good kind of discomfort. When I was a young singer, I was constantly looking to others for validation: my teachers, the audience, anyone who listened. At midlife, there's no juice in the prizes I once longed to have. I sense my path moving in a new direction towards serving a higher purpose.

It's only recently that I'm beginning to truly appreciate and value the journey to mastery. I know that giving me answers to the most important questions of my life won't make me any more competent at living. It will just give me solutions which, if they don't turn out, could lead me to blame someone else (perhaps my coach this time) for what doesn't work in my life.

Getting unstuck requires I start seeing myself as smart and capable of developing whatever competencies I need for my next career. I'm grateful to have a competent coach who has mastered the process of living itself and can help me stay on track.

Now what will my coach ask of me? And how will he keep me present to what I need to do to improve my performance and help me grow?

COMMITMENTS

Silence is like an empty dance floor for our thoughts. With gentle coaxing, each idea gets a turn to come to the center and be run through its paces.

My schedule, normally packed solid, doesn't allow much time for reflection. At my coach's suggestion, I'm on a weekend getaway alone at a local retreat. Taking time out has been the best thing I could do right now. Peaceful walks alone in nature, hours of silence in this monastic environment, and long nights of sleep are leaving me feeling refreshed and clear. I'm coming back to my coach with a possible purpose and a heartfelt commitment to make a difference with the rest of my life.

Interestingly, that purpose has little to do with what I've been focusing on or doing so far. In seeking to identify my highest goal, the goal that fills my heart with joyful song, I've had to think beyond my past accomplishments, failures, and disappointments.

I've had to dream again.

But the dream has shifted. I'm different these last few days. Maybe this is part of a midlife transition, some phenomenon tied to growing older. My coach confirms my suspicion and affirms my choice.

I no longer see my life as being about what I want others or the world to give me. I now long for it to be about giving the best of who I am to help others expand their influence. Specifically, I want to help leaders communicate more effectively to create positive change in the world.

This new commitment to a higher purpose feels right for me—and at the same time, totally uncertain and very risky. The chances of failure seem greater than anything I've taken on before. The thought of success in this inspires me to grow and learn, to become someone I have not yet been.

All of a sudden, I've raised the stakes in my game.

MEETING GINI

Clarifying our purpose—the contribution we want to make now and in the future—helps focus our attention, time, and energy on what's most important to us. As I start talking with Gini Dalgas, I'm intrigued by the synchronicity that connected her to her coach, and I'm reminded that conversations about purpose are essential to shaping the design of our coaching.

> Gini Dalgas was listening to an internationally renowned professional mountain biker address students in Canmore, Alberta. This world-class athlete, visiting Banff as part of a biking film festival, had offered to visit several of the local schools while in the area. Gini's admiration and respect grew as she watched him adjust his presentation to meet the needs of this particular young audience—using his biking prowess and reputation to inspire and encourage them to be responsible for bringing their unique talents, gifts, and abilities into the world. That encouragement was not lost on Gini.
>
> She was at a personal crossroads in terms of her participation with the Canmore Community Cruisers, a local nonprofit bike share society she had helped found several years earlier with five other people. With his connections to biking and community, this thirty-year-old athlete seemed like a natural choice to coach her around her commitment to the Cruisers. So when an opportunity to do so appeared, she took it without hesitation.
>
> "Coaching wasn't about having to change my life, as if I'd been doing something wrong. I really liked that. It

was working on some 'wish' things and how to make that happen in a slow and steady way."

Gini Dalgas, Canmore Community Cruisers

Her intention going in wasn't to make big changes. Nor was it to have her coach give her a "plan" for developing her biking skills, like when she had been coached in high school basketball and water polo. It was about creating a way forward so she could be more successful in realizing her commitment to help the Cruisers grow and have a bigger impact.

In the past, Gini had ideas about how to do this, but no matter what she had done, things didn't seem to move forward as quickly or as easily as she would have liked. When she first started working with her coach, she was wondering if this was even the right way for her to be spending her time and energy. So they began by looking at whether she was really still committed to the Society.

Gini's account reminds me of how I felt just before meeting my coach. My strategies weren't working, and I had begun to doubt the viability of what I was trying to do. Hanging out in this place of, "It's not working and I don't know what to do about it," was uncomfortable, and I had been starting to lean towards giving up.

Normally a cup half full person, Gini had been feeling the cup was half empty with the Cruisers. Her predisposition to work hard for what she believes in—even if others aren't interested— had served her well so far. Gini normally operated like a lone tree planter in a clear-cut. But when it came to the Cruisers, that approach hadn't delivered results.

Lone tree planter in a clear-cut. That sounds similar to my identifying with superwoman. Unfortunately, my "powers" have the unsettling habit of wearing off. The spell keeps breaking, making it harder and harder for me to continue believing in the value of being an independent superheroine.

Through conversations with her coach, Gini came to see that the Society was important to her and to accept that she was overwhelmed by a seemingly insurmountable mountain of obstacles. She also realized that having a bigger impact happens *with others*, and that she could choose to remain a relative soloist or become the leader of a team of people with unique talents, abilities, and strengths who shared her commitment to making biking accessible. Organizations—especially community-based ones—succeed through group effort and leadership from at least one committed individual.

"I think we all have that lonely tree planter feeling at some time in our life, with something that we are interested in and feel strongly about. There's a strength there. But you do need the collective and need to figure out how to be a collective on things too. And welcome people into your idea."

Gini Dalgas

Gini chose to step up and carry the vision forward.

Being clear about what you're up to as an individual focuses your choices and actions. Apply this to helping a group of individuals articulate what they're trying to accomplish together, and you'd have the makings of a strong foundation for collaboration.

With her commitment clarified, Gini and her coach focused on what was missing for the Cruisers to grow: a compelling vision and specific requests for help. Gini found herself calling on her coach to help her think as a leader about this. Used to optimistically jumping in and doing things quickly by herself, she now took time to think her ideas through strategically and to fully consider what was needed, who and what might be impacted, and what other people's interests and concerns might be. At her coach's invitation, she began having conversations with specific individuals in the community about her ideas regarding what the

Society could be doing, noticing their reactions, gathering their feedback and input, and incorporating it all into her thinking.

Having conversations with people who shared her perspective was easy for Gini. Starting a conversation with someone whose opinion differed from hers was not. Her coach revealed that these seemingly challenging conversations have the potential to transform relationships and disclose information that can be critical to success. She then began working with him on developing some skill in collaborative dialogue.

My coach has talked with me about developing the skill of listening in a way that leaves space for people to freely share their perspective. I've been starting to practice this listening with curiosity, listening without judgment. It's not always easy. When I feel the urge to jump in and save the day by sharing my opinion or giving advice, I've been telling myself to act as if I have laryngitis. This helps me keep my mouth shut and reengage my curiosity to listen to the other person's perspective—until I have something critical to contribute that will help move the conversation forward.

Gini practiced first with those she had no resistance to speaking with, gradually learning how to create a natural back-and-forth flow in which people share their perspectives on an issue without feeling the need to justify and uphold their particular point of view. When her coach began to prompt her to set up meetings with key people about her vision for the Cruisers, she resisted, making up excuses that she hadn't yet mastered collaborative dialogue.

Her commitment called. Bikes in the community were worth talking about—whether or not she felt she was ready to talk.

Gini's coach gave her another assignment: to watch the movie *Anchorman*.[2] When she did, she connected with the competent, professional female protagonist trying to be taken seriously in a male-dominated industry. As a middle-aged woman who rides beater bikes and who isn't a good mechanic, Gini had sensed something was at play in the background of some of her conversations. Her coach, twenty years her junior, helped her see the challenge she was facing by stepping up to lead the conversation in a male-oriented biking community. The metaphor of being the calm, capable anchorwoman appealed to her, and it soon became a touchstone in her coaching process.

So we can choose a new metaphor for ourselves when our old way of being has us stuck and unable to take care of what we care about. Hmmm. So I could ditch the superwoman identity for something else. I wonder how the calm, capable anchorwoman metaphor worked for Gini.

Gini chose to stay with her commitment and speak about what she thought would be good for everyone in the community. She started having collaborative conversations with people who had diverse points of view. She listened to their ideas and used them to enhance and inform her own thinking about a new vision for the Cruisers. She recruited several new people onto the Society's Board. She took time to craft a clear message. And then she held a strategic planning meeting with the Board to look at the original purpose and core values of the Society and how those had changed, as well as her suggestion for a possible new vision and how that might be realized.

Rather than focus only on a commitment to share bikes, the Community Cruisers could respond to the need to get affordable bikes into the community. Through subsidies and connecting people with available bikes, they could move from spending all their time and energy on finding missing bikes and fixing broken ones to providing an affordable transportation alternative for community members. And through community engagement events and workshops, they could teach people about the value of bikes and how to maintain them.

"We want people to see bikes as a vehicle, an affordable source of transportation, and to value bikes as a resource so they take good care of them. So if they see a bike in a creek bed, they might give it to us—knowing that even if we can't repair it, we will strip off useful parts for someone else in the community."

Gini Dalgas

The Board agreed to test these ideas and explore opportunities to collaborate with other community organizations in supporting biking as a viable transportation alternative. Sharing their clear, positive, progressive message, they have begun consulting with local bike shops (including the local thrift shop which resells used bikes), biking clubs, and the municipal waste management authorities. They are also gathering input from the whole community at public events about ideas such as having a seasonal workshop space where residents can go to work on their bikes and, for a nominal fee, have access to tools and mentors.

Gini's commitment to being the anchorwoman seems to have generated more inclusion and sharing, more working *with* others.

"We are part of a collective still. It's easy to forget that when you get really passionate. You can't be just a part of the collective and keep moving forward. It takes some individuality and a connection to the collective to move an idea that is for the good of all forward. You need both."

Gini Dalgas

Having met the challenge to commit to becoming a more collaborative leader, Gini is no longer being a lone tree planter trying to move the Cruisers' work forward at breakneck speed. She's created her own effortless way to lead—a way that feels natural and easy. She is comfortable with letting go of ideas that don't interest others; comfortable with doing a few strategic things each year, doing them well, and getting better each time;

comfortable with taking the time to enroll and collaborate with people committed to positive change. When it comes to the Community Cruisers, Gini now feels as if she's out on a long mountain hike in magnificent terrain with colleagues, and that even if they get caught in a thunderstorm, their work will be fine. They're all in it together.

I'm inspired by Gini's choice to reengage with her commitment to the Cruisers. And I'm intrigued by how shifting who she was being—consciously committing to living a new metaphor for herself—took care of what she cares about and made effective collaboration possible.

REFLECTING

We are fully committed all the time. We live in a sea of commitments. Some float into conscious awareness, like my declared commitment to work with a coach. Others may remain below the surface of consciousness, like a hidden commitment to being "right" or to not being hurt again. During a coaching relationship, we can observe our conscious and unconscious commitments, their impact on our lives, and whether they connect with our purpose. If we're not clear about our purpose, we might explore that with our coach. With this information, we then can freely choose how we want to continue relating to each of our commitments: we can change them, revoke them, renegotiate them, or recommit to them.

When, like Gini, we choose commitments that we don't know how to realize, we often find ourselves facing a somewhat uncomfortable gap between where and who we are now and where and who we need to be in order to fulfill that goal. We can look at this as an opportunity to try on a new way of being.

Great coaches stand for you, committed yet unattached, as you undertake this process of "becoming." Perhaps our highest goal in life is to experience our connection to the amazing possibility we are—all the time. As Michael Ray mentions in his book *The Highest Goal,* our potentiality is like the shimmering blue pearl of light described in some spiritual traditions.

The "blue pearl" is, perhaps, an apt metaphor for what coaches see in their clients, and what they help clients see for themselves. The metaphor points to what a coaching relationship can achieve: the coming into existence of the possibility we are. The coach's job is not to measure the probability of whether who we are *as a possibility* is being fully realized, but to guide us as we learn to access our inherent capacity for growth and development in the lifelong journey of self-realization. The choice rests with us as to what aspects of the blue pearl of our potentiality we commit to realizing at any point in our lives.

This can open up whole new areas of questions and possibilities. What's the gap between how we're showing up in the world now and how we need to be showing up to fulfill our commitments? What's the identity we need to create in order to be credible? How can we behave and interact with others like the person we intend to become in whatever we're doing now?

> "We observe your current approach—your way of being—and integrate the best of it into a new way of being that will better serve your goals. This new approach will have new skills, new competencies, new muscles that, over time, will become embodied and sustainable. You can't build a coaching relationship by following protocol. If the process is too stiff or structured, I might miss 'You.' One has to come from a place of presence and openness."
>
> Ryan Leech

It's no surprise that much of the work in coaching occurs between sessions. When you start paying attention to your way of being, everything in your life can become part of your evolution. You see yourself as a player in the development of yourself as a player. You take on the challenge of establishing new habits, new ways of observing, thinking, and responding. Observing how eager you are to take on assignments from your coach, how willing you are to consider new perspectives, and how much resistance you have about trying new actions can reveal to you the intangible shifts taking place in your way of being.

Effective coaches help their clients set up measurable goals that relate to their commitments. Coaching to a new way of being, done in service of fulfilling commitments, still needs to produce results. We can measure progress by clarifying goals and setting up a scoreboard. Coaches can use the scoreboard as an ongoing frame of reference. However, coachees can put it aside to focus on playing the game they've set up, trusting they can revisit the scoreboard at any time and they don't need to watch it constantly.

> "You have to figure out a way to have quantitative and qualitative results, and bring some rigor to those without losing the spirit of what coaching is. Coaching is not based in a plan, predict, and control model. It is truly a sense, commit, create together approach."
>
> Dr. Carolyn Hendrickson

When we focus on our game, we become more conscious in each moment of our habitual ways of responding to the world. We can be more present to what drives our choices. For example, if our old way of being was to commit to things we knew we'd never do, perhaps our new way includes having a high rate of follow-through on our promises. Attentiveness to our way of being allows for more conscious choices, which allows for different results.

In highly successful coaching relationships, both coach and coachee commit to co-creating the relationship. Coaching isn't about controlling the client's development. It's about respecting and helping clarify the coachee's connection to their inner guidance and fostering that connection consistently. Transformational coaches, in particular, will create an environment of trust in which people can choose who they are being, who they are becoming, and in what ways they want to fully express themselves in the world.

"There's a sacred space that's created when a client and I engage in a commitment together. It is a strong and solid space regardless of the form, regardless of the number of hours we're on the phone or in person together over the course of several months to several years. The form helps support something. The amount of progress the client makes is not contingent or dependent upon the form. They sign a contract and they're in a 'field' with me that we're creating with our intention."

Virginia Rhoads, Jempe Center

This co-commitment to a co-created sacred space benefits the coachee directly in terms of their development and indirectly through their coach's development.

Coaches receive by giving. They are enriched by a coachee's growth. Just as teachers grow by teaching, coaches grow by coaching. Every coaching conversation gives the coach an opportunity to revisit their own assumptions, distinctions, and ways of being. To see possibilities and connections they hadn't seen before makes it possible for them to contribute even more to their client.

"You know things are cooking when you're co-creating a conversation. In the beginning, you're asking questions and having them see things they maybe didn't see, including how they observe and interpret the world. If we can see the world differently, we're able to take actions we couldn't see with the previous view. When it gets powerful is when that's happening mutually—when I start seeing things I didn't see with regards to them or their business. It's almost like an authentic, 'sacred' space."

Tim Seeton, Paracomm International

Effective coaches commit to their own ongoing development. They know the importance of not having their ego, their attachments, or any unmet expectations interfere with the coaching. Coaches with commitments to enhancing self-awareness and engaging in self-development will be less likely to enter into a coaching engagement that is a poor fit—where core values are misaligned or it's not possible to genuinely embrace the client's goals—or to pull focus away from the client's agenda. To coach being conscious of your own mindset, belief system, and core values can be likened to coaching "clean."

> "It starts with me. I have to do the work: the self-inquiry to discover who I am. From there, I can be of more service to others."
>
> Ryan Leech

Almost all the coaches I spoke with either have coaches of their own, trusted peers they can turn to for ad hoc coaching, or a trusted advisor or mentor who can point to their blind spots. Many continue to develop themselves through programs or in conversations with others about their learning edge.

> "When I'm tending to my personal work, my clients start having breakthroughs. I know I'm in a great coaching relationship with a client when I find myself sharing something I've just learned in the last forty-eight hours about myself—my own growth, my journey, somewhere I've created a huge mess and consequently a new doorway. I know I'm in flow with that particular client when making sense of myself can come out in the coaching conversation. They won't always know that I'm sharing about a specific situation I've navigated, but often they do."
>
> Virginia Rhoads

When coaches work "clean," they are authentically themselves, unassuming and honest about their strengths, open with their vulnerability, unabashed about their authentic commitment to the coachee, and listening to *their* inner guidance. Not only do they model what's possible, but they also can bring this integrity to the sacred space of the coaching relationship.

In a world of more than 6 billion people, a coach's way of being and self-awareness benefits their clients. It can also distinguish them from the people we forget. Memorable coaches influence who we choose to be and help us shape who we're known to be (our identity in the world).

INTEGRATING

I have a sense my coach is probably one of those memorable people. Already he has helped me clarify my highest purpose: to develop myself so that I can help leaders create positive change in the world. His calm confidence in me, in my capacity to close my gap and become who I need to be to fulfill that goal, reassures me that I don't need to waste time living someone else's life.

When the going gets tough, I can come back to my overarching commitment and his belief in me.

With my highest purpose clarified, what obstacles might remain between me and its realization?

> No man ever achieved worthwhile success who did not, at one time or other, find himself with at least one foot hanging well over the brink of failure.
>
> Napoleon Hill[1]

DISCOMFORT

Networking is my least favorite activity in life—after shopping. For a self-confessed introvert, talking to people about who I am and what I offer is almost as painful as having an endometrial biopsy (men, think prostate exam). Yet I know introducing myself to new people is essential to my success. My network so far includes only a few leaders who want to create positive change.

I'm uncomfortably stuck and I need help to get unstuck.

My coach is adamant that it's natural to fear failure. He shares an old adage with me: fail often, fail fast, fail cheap. The saying makes it sound as if failure is something great—as if it's something I can dance with—maybe something even greater than success. I'm not sure about this. I thought my coach was going to help me be successful. Not teach me how to fail. Yet, as I hang up after our coaching call, I sense something disquieting in what he's saying, something about my relationship to failure.

For weeks now, I've felt like Jonathan Livingston Seagull— uncomfortably poised at the edge of a cliff, one foot suspended in midair, uncertain whether I'll plummet to the ground or take off in flight. I have a list of people to call and I haven't called anyone yet. Here I am, afraid of being hurt, one foot glued to the cliff, holding on for dear life to the certainty that comes with not trying. Avoiding rejection, cheating death. But no risk taking also means I'll never get what I want. No risk taking guarantees I'll never succeed.

In trying to avoid failure, I've risked success.

I've failed beautifully.

The question is what will I do now? If I don't risk failing, I'll never learn what doesn't work. And if I never learn what doesn't work, I'll never discover what my full potential might be. I'll never learn if I can really succeed in business—and in life.

I'm pulling out my list of contacts.

I have nothing to lose by jumping off the cliff.

MEETING DENISE

Each interview I do for this book feels like jumping off another cliff. Every conversation is another move into my discomfort, another step towards a breakthrough. Little did I know this morning that talking with Denise Rundle would entirely change how I feel about playing outside my comfort zone.

> Five years ago, Denise was a successful, high-achieving senior leader at Microsoft®. Having a coach indicated you were on the upswing in your career, so she decided to try it out when it came up in discussion with her boss about her work development plan.
>
> Several years earlier, Denise had made a decision which was a lingering issue for her—a decision that had led to consequences that didn't fit with her almost spotless high-achiever record. Sales of a new product had been phenomenally higher than anticipated, and she had not arranged to have sufficient people in place to handle the demand for customer service support. As the leader accountable for ensuring key products were sufficiently supported globally, she had dropped the ball. Denise was determined this would never happen again. So in 2007, when the next new product was launched, she had everything in place to ensure customers would not wait long for service.
>
> It was at this time that she began working with her coach. Her unconscious goal going in was to prove that she was already a fabulous, emotionally grounded, smart, and capable leader. After

nine months of working together, she had a breakthrough. A rock climbing session with her coach opened her up to some of the most profound learning in her coaching relationship.

Initially reticent to waste time climbing walls, Denise rationalized the experience as a way to multitask: combine a workout and a coaching session and check both off her list for the day. At the bottom of the first wall, fully equipped with her gear, she looked up, assessed the situation, and announced that she probably wouldn't be able to do much because of an old knee injury. Her coach invited her to be open to the possibilities.

Surprisingly, she climbed the wall in almost no time. She went on to the next one, and the next. Finally, she found herself standing in front of a wall and thinking, "I wish I could do that, but I know I can't." When her coach asked if she wanted to try it, she told him what she thought. He invited her again to be open to the possibilities and pointed out that her story about not being able to climb was just that—a story—and she didn't actually know what her limit was. So she climbed this final wall, reaching the top with little difficulty. When they were done, her coach pointed out two things. Denise had thought her limit was the first wall. At the end of the day, she still didn't know what her limit was.

I remember hearing the little voice in my head screaming, "No way!" when my yoga teacher led me into a new posture yesterday. Breathing into my fear, I kept moving and gracefully completed the pose (to my surprise and delight). My teacher's insight at the end of our class: "The ego always shows up on the mat. One never knows when or what will trigger it…but you can be sure it will appear."

Insight flooded Denise: in trying to avoid failure at all costs, she had been playing a small game. And how we are with one thing is how we are with everything. She was working on just the things she knew she could manage and keep safe. She had failed to push herself to take risks.

"There are very few moments of failure in my life. But this failure was that I wasn't pushing myself and taking risks. To the outside world, it would look like I was because I was a successful partner in the company. But I wasn't living up to my potential. I didn't know what my potential was. I just didn't—for fear. My definition of success had been 'not failing.'"

Denise Rundle, General Manager, Microsoft Corporation

I've been using Denise's definition: *success equals "not failing."* Yet, when I think about all the people I call "successful," they've experienced their fair share of mistakes, breakdowns, losses, and disappointments.

Denise realized two things: her focus on keeping a clean scorecard had blinded her to the fact that this latest new product was not a bestseller in the marketplace, and proving herself and getting her coach's approval was not what coaching was all about. She had been playing to the gallery—specifically, to her bosses and her coach—and organizing her energy around getting approval and recognition. Realizing this was not allowing her to be on track with her unique purpose, she made a commitment to face her anxiety and look at how she was really showing up in the world.

It was time to focus on mastering her game as a player.

Denise stopped "faking" her coaching sessions and, in spite of her discomfort around looking at her blind spots and gaps as a leader, she invited her coach to do a 360 assessment to reveal "the good, the bad, and the ugly." Her coach and his wife, who is also an executive coach, conducted interviews with senior leaders in Denise's organization and observed her in action to see and hear what it was really like working for and with this gold star performer. Both coaches helped her take in the collective feedback without feeling shame for any past mistakes or failures.

The three of them then met with her team to share a summary of what they had discovered, and to make sure Denise was accurately interpreting what people had reported. The coaching couple then used what they had learned to help design a way forward with one-on-one and two-on-one coaching interactions that could close the gaps and help Denise become an even better leader.

I sense that 360-degree assessments could be like biopsies: intrusive, sometimes painful, uncomfortable. Yet, done well, they can reveal to us what we cannot or have not wanted to see: our habitual behaviors, patterned responses, and self-limiting stories. What has become transparent to us.

"For the sake of what are you willing to push through any of the discomfort and face that you might not be perfect? To really realize my potential as a human being, I had to face that discomfort."

Denise Rundle

Denise's authentic openness and genuine desire for self-improvement made this process a powerful turning point. As the leader of her group, she began requesting of the experts on her team that they make sure she had the benefit of *their* expertise informing her decisions. Rather than simply focusing on being an exceptional executor, Denise started to listen for and discern opportunities to contribute the depth of her experience to the senior executive team. She listened to her peers to learn from the breadth of their experience, and she looked for how her vision and aspirations fit into the bigger picture to begin to sense what her potential as a leader might be.

I'm intrigued to hear that, after facing the discomfort of receiving the 360 feedback with her coaches, Denise began to more openly invite and listen for the perspectives and expertise of her peers and colleagues. It seems as if the fantastic space of a coaching relationship can be a testing ground for transparent, open dialogue. Denise brings me up short as she starts to talk about choosing a new definition of success.

> For her, success would be leaving a professional and personal legacy that makes a positive difference. As her vision grew, Denise became more intentional about what she wanted her impact to be in every area of her life: in the industry, in the marketplace, for her customers, for her peers and her team, for her parents and her children. Rather than be on autopilot and end up wasting time on things that weren't important to her, she chose to plan her impact a full year in advance, starting with scheduling time for things she must do (but hates) and allocating time for things that will make a meaningful difference (including what she does herself and what she delegates). Once 95 percent of her calendar was filled with professional and personal things, she reviewed it to make sure she had left *at most* 5 percent for urgent, unimportant things. The discipline and rigor of this process delivered an exponential increase in her impact at work.

I can hear this focus in Denise's speaking. I can only imagine the results she achieves by having every day intentionally designed to contribute to what she cares about. Not that Denise has to play the perfect superhero now.

> When crises or breakdowns happen, she reassesses her commitments, intentions, and time allocations and makes adjustments. In addition, her coach has helped her connect with more of the uncomfortable physical and physiological aspects of being a human leader. Denise has improved her ability to observe without judgment her body's natural response to a stressful situation (be it fight, freeze, or flight), developed techniques for managing her physical responses in stressful situations so that she can stay open and connected, and shifted her relationship to anxiety.

> "Anxiety is a human condition: it's normal. Believe it or not, many leaders operate as if they are supposed to be

superhuman. It helps to know other people are human and only expect you to be human too."

Denise Rundle

I can see how coaching can help us increase our mindfulness and give us the possibility of no longer being at the mercy of triggers and old definitions of success. Yet, simply seeing what we've been blind to, in and of itself, doesn't change anything. It's what we do with our new awareness in action with people that counts. I listen with admiration as Denise finishes her story.

> Coaching has had an incredible impact on Denise's life and on the lives of those around her. Not only has she become a better, more impactful leader, but she has also invested in one-on-one coaching for members of her team and participated in group coaching sessions with them. Her entire leadership team now shares a common language and approach to things. Extended family members of employees have thanked her for investing in their loved one's success and happiness. And above all, in service of her commitment to make a positive difference, Denise continues to open up to work on whatever is next in the realm of "beyond safe."

As I thank Denise for her contribution to this book and to me with this conversation, I'm left wondering where else I might be avoiding failing in my life. Where else do I play for the comfort of approval? Where else do I stop myself before I even try?

REFLECTING

Our natural tendency as human beings to avoid discomfort can interfere with getting the coaching we need. When our fear of being uncomfortable overrides our commitment to getting results, instinct can have us gravitate towards playing it safe and selecting a coach who won't be too hard on us.

"People confuse wanting to be comfortable with getting a result. There are any number of people out there who need coaches they don't select. They select someone who's not actually going to help them. This person is not going to be that hard on me. They're not going to hit me over the head about the stupid things I do so that I stop doing them. I can perpetuate this false sense of myself and blame all these other people for what's going on in my life and play the victim forever and wonder why I'm not fulfilled."

Michael McDermott

Being coached by someone you connect with, someone you like and really want to be with, is important. Being approved of or acknowledged by your coach can boost your self-confidence and create relationship. However, relying too heavily on connection, acknowledgment, and approval when selecting a coach can limit our success. And, unfortunately, going for easy leaves us still carrying around our old baggage. If we've truly committed to having our life work, best to look for a coach with the capacity and competency to be tough with us—and to be there for us when the going gets tough.

"I don't care if you don't feel comfortable. If you wait to feel comfortable, you'll probably never take action. Being uncomfortable is probably a good thing."

Tim Seeton

Great coaches can accurately read our physiological experience and sense our feelings and moods. Going "beyond safe" can have strong somatic and emotional components. Some coaches have developed a heightened awareness or sensitivity to other people's emotional states. Others bring specialized training in kinesthetic awareness, nonverbal communication, acting, voice, or physiology to their work. Sometimes these coaches can be even more aware than we are of what's going on with us.

"I take into account what's happening with my client and myself somatically. I notice unconscious somatic patterns they have, certain movements they make when they're talking about specific topics, and may bring that into the conversation."

Ryan Leech

Fear, for example, a natural response to any perceived threat, can show up in coaching interactions. Many things trigger fear: uncertainty, perceived danger, persistent anxiety about the future, the necessity to speak in public. Coaching doesn't look to heal past experiences—especially traumatic ones—that may have conditioned us to be fearful. That's the domain of the qualified therapist. Coaches help us look to see where our automatic physiological responses have us repeatedly fighting, freezing, or fleeing.

"Fear drives wild behaviors if we don't learn to manage our reactions in response to its presence within us. We need to become more reflective, to sit and tolerate the tension of silence long enough to connect with our values, to think more systemically and consider the impact of our actions."

Kim Loop, Human Systems Renewal

Great coaches can be with our discomfort and help us move through it. The passage through discomfort can begin in many ways. It may start like Denise's did, with a relatively "safe" experience on a climbing wall. It may occur quietly over time, like gradually awakening to the fact that we have an addiction to work. Or we may find ourselves suddenly knocked off center by a medical crisis, the loss of a job, or the death of a loved one. No matter where we begin, great coaches challenge us to step outside our comfort zone and face our underlying fears and concerns.

"Coaching is not about comfort. So if someone calls me and says it won't be comfortable or convenient to come at a certain time, I won't take them as a client. If they think that life must be comfortable, it's not my client. If they say they can't, they have another appointment, that's okay. Comfort is not important. Achievement is much more important."

Anabella Shaked

Great coaches can accurately sense what's going on with us, throw the ball to where we want to be, and then vigilantly have us rise to the occasion. They have the fortitude to be with us through the hard times and the boring times. Their unreasonableness can help us get to where our old scripts fall away and we can discover what's on the other side of it all.

Effective coaches help us observe our automatic responses and behaviors without judgment—so we can choose differently if we wish. Our habitual responses can keep us trapped inside our own stories, perpetually playing out old dramas. We may have identified ourselves in the past as superheroes anxiously fighting, serial quitters fleeing, or stuck people floating in mediocrity. Sometimes, we may have demonstrated all of these responses simultaneously, although in different domains of our lives. Coaches can help us learn to observe not only what triggers our old scripts, but also the consequences our habitual behaviors have on our well-being, relationships, and effectiveness in the world.

"The coachee has to be willing to look at things that are sometimes not comfortable to look at: areas of their life and their work where they're not doing well, where they could do better, or where they might have blind spots— a way of being in a leadership role or in a partnership or in their life that has been contributing to the mess or the lack of satisfaction. They are asked to look at beliefs and assumptions they hold and to consider whether these beliefs no longer serve them. Even though the value on the other side of that discomfort is extraordinary, it's sometimes difficult while it's happening. The coachee has to be willing to look, to experience, to be uncomfortable."

Virginia Rhoads

Exposing our blind spots doesn't change anything. It's what we do with our new awareness that counts. We can develop practices to increase our mindfulness so that we're no longer at the mercy of triggers, instinct, or hidden drives. And then, with our coaches, we can go one step further: we can move to take new actions and respond differently—in spite of our discomfort.

"Life is movement. Either you're expanding and learning or you're contracting. We're either growing or we're dying. The real power in life is to expand. To be willing to tolerate what's there and to include it, to work with it in a way that doesn't resist it or defend a point of view, to grow and learn from it."

Marcia Martin

Moving into action challenges, stimulates, pulls, and prods us to grow. Audacious coaches who can keep holding our feet to the fire prove invaluable when we're creating new neuronal pathways, developing new habits, opening up to failure, testing our limits.

Effective coaches can accurately identify what's interfering with our being successful. We may claim any number of things in our circumstances or background have blocked us from realizing our full potential. Coaches will take these into consideration but will not be swayed by our story about them. Their contribution to us will more likely take the form of surfacing and working with outdated playbooks, recurring moods (such as anxiety, anger, fear, frustration, resignation, or boredom) and tendencies (such as self-consciousness, self-doubt, perfectionism, attachment to being right, or acting out unconscious commitments). Any of these aspects of our way of being may unconsciously pervade our presence and undermine our ability to enroll and work with others.

Effective coaches can also identify what we're missing to be successful. They share any critical gaps they see in our competencies and knowledge that we need to close. When we lack clarity, they can act as a partner in thinking our way through the situation we're in. When we doubt ourselves, they can invoke and help us develop our self-trust. When we falter, they can invite us to revisit our purpose and commitments. And when we fail, they can help us discover what we need to learn from our experience.

> "Churchill said 'Success is being able to go from failure to failure without losing enthusiasm.' And that has been my motto. I find that true with my clients. The only real tragedy is to not learn from a mistake. That's the relationship I cultivate for myself and my clients if they haven't identified it that way."
>
> Madeleine Homan Blanchard, Blanchard Certified

Coachees who find coaching particularly effective use their coach's contributions to stay fully present to all aspects of their game. They don't shy away from working in areas that their coach identifies for accelerated learning and growth. They openly explore the interrelationships in all domains of their life. They put aside their discomfort with being vulnerable to weave their well-being, mood, finances, failures, challenges, and relationships into their coaching conversations. And they don't withhold information that could help their coach succeed.

INTEGRATING

Coming from a performing background, I thought I knew what it meant to be vulnerable. After all, I bared my emotions, my heart, my soul in every performance. But they were just performances—not my "real" life.

Having my life work—really work—demands that I allow my coach to come in close, see my true nature, and reflect it back to me. I'm not sure I've allowed anyone in my life so far to "see" me in this way.

I'm not sure I've allowed *myself* to see myself this intimately.

And so I'm now choosing to adopt a definition of success, said to belong to The Body Shop® founder Anita Roddick, that will demand that I am this honest, this vulnerable with myself and my coach. A definition that allows me to live authentically.

From now on, success is "shaping my own destiny."

Where in my life will this show up first?

> "I am responsible. I have the courage to live life from profound integrity. I am my word."
>
> Jim Selman

RESPONSIBILITY

Talk about pushing my buttons. My coach suggests I'm not being responsible for my relationships. I tell him I see it differently.

I *am* "the responsible one"!

Admittedly, I've been complaining to him—and others—about what's not working in my primary relationship and speaking negatively about my ability to have intimacy in my life.

I grew up with the idea that love came from being responsible for my younger twin sisters. From the age of three, love appeared to me to be the reward for helping take care of their safety and well-being before my own. Caring for others was a roundabout way of taking care of my needs for attention and acknowledgment. "Others first" became a habit, the way I oriented myself in relationships. I gained approval and recognition as "the responsible daughter." And this old habit has me wallowing in muddy feelings about what's happening today.

My coach has a different definition of being responsible in relationships. For him, "being responsible" has no implied obligation of duty or reward: it is simply having the ability to respond and choosing to do so.

With this new definition of responsibility, I can see that my mediocre performance with reaching out and connecting to new people has been irresponsible. I've been worrying, "What if all these new people call on me? How can I take care of all of them? I can only handle so much at a time." So I've just been drifting along, convinced I'm better off not initiating new conversations and leaning instead on a few close colleagues to introduce me to people *they* know and trust.

I'm making a conscious choice to act differently from now on. I will be responsible for being impeccable in what I say. I'll be in integrity. No more complaining to others. No more speaking against myself.

I will be 100 percent responsible for every relationship in my life. I'll consciously design my new relationships, renegotiate existing ones to work well, and let go of old ones that don't have juice left in them.

I get to choose in each moment what and how much I'm willing to be responsible for—without being afraid I'll have to give more than I have the capacity for in any relationship.

MEETING MICHAEL

Devoting myself to a "stretch assignment" like this is a risk worth taking—especially if I'm truly committed to growth and success. The saying, "You create your own opportunities," comes to mind as I wait for Michael Rosen to join me. The timelessness of this platitude seems somehow reassuring as I settle in to listen to this successful senior executive tell me about his first coaching experience.

> Michael had just been promoted to president of the Background Screening Division of Marsh & McLennan, a Fortune 100 risk and insurance services firm. A lawyer by trade, he had over twenty years experience in the risk mitigation industry. He had co-founded Background America, Inc., a US-based start-up, which was acquired by Kroll®, a global leader in risk mitigation and response, and which then merged with Marsh & McLennan. For Michael, stepping into this new position to lead one thousand employees, including many of his former colleagues, was going to be a stretch in more ways than one.

> His new leadership responsibilities included developing a strategy and expanding the division's business globally while keeping their regulatory and compliance technology at the leading edge. His first objective was to create and restate what the company vision

was in seven different cultures for employees in as many different countries. The challenge: Michael had no experience in international business and he was not a technologist. Realizing he needed help, he pursued the recommendation of a trusted colleague and met with an executive coach.

"I knew nothing about coaching. I thought it was life skills or had something to do with a psychologist. I had the wrong impression: it was none of those. My coach was able to draw things out in a business way. No one had been able to do that for me or had been able to ask and challenge me in a way in which I was willing to be probed. And it worked very well."

Michael Rosen, President & Co-founder, ProviderTrust Inc.

My networking challenge felt like a mountain—until now. The fact that Michael responded to the challenges of his new leadership responsibilities by finding an executive coach reminds me that we can safely involve others we trust in our stretch.

Encouraged by the coach's demeanor and disposition, Michael decided to start working with him on three immediate concerns. First, Michael expected he wouldn't be able to succeed in this new position without a background in technology and international business. Second, he anticipated that the people who had been working with him for ten years would have certain expectations of him that would make it difficult to engage them in shifting the culture in their company. And third, his team expected him to handle an unresolved issue with one of their members in a particular way, and when he didn't, they openly bet against him.

"I didn't hire my coach to come in and tell me I did a great job. We set out specific things that I needed to work on."

Michael Rosen

I sense great clarity and commitment from Michael. A commitment to being coached and a commitment to get what he needs from coaching so that he can fulfill his responsibility for the success of his division.

> The first thing Michael noticed was that whenever he was in a coaching conversation, he was really being "heard." Rather than just listen to Michael talk, his coach would interject and restate the issue and the underlying concern he was hearing. Sometimes what he heard didn't match what Michael was thinking, so they'd talk about better ways of saying what he was trying to communicate. A gradual back-and-forth dialogue helped clarify exactly what they needed to explore in their coaching and opened their conversations up to looking at what was holding this high achiever back from being even more successful on the global stage.

My coach—like Michael's—has this impressive ability to identify where I'm stuck, what's not working, and where I'm not communicating what I mean.

> Together, they looked at perspectives Michael had not yet seen or considered valid. They explored the viewpoint that his extensive knowledge of background screening was all he really needed to know to begin leading, and that he could hire the best people he could find to create a strong, balanced team. They considered that people may want their leaders to change things up so their company can grow, and that they may even want their leader to fight their battles for them with the corporates in head office.

> With his coach probing, challenging, and guiding him, Michael began to acknowledge and play to his strengths. He stopped worrying and focused his attention on adding value. Instead of expecting to be everybody's best friend, he made the tough decisions and initiated the difficult conversations that would help the business grow. He learned how to work with the corporates in head office—standing up for his people, managing a $100 million operation as smoothly as possible, and, occasionally,

making mistakes.

One day Michael received a call from the CEO, asking if he would travel immediately to the UK to terminate a member of his operations team. Although Michael had been alerted to this employee's power-hungry behaviors and questionable intentions, he responded by saying he was on vacation with his family and offered to get to it the following week. His assumption that this across-the-pond management issue could wait until he was ready to deal with it was incorrect: the CEO handled it himself the next day.

I see another connection to responsibility here. I may be committed to being coached. My coach and I may both be committed and responsible for our coaching relationship. But it's me—and me alone—who is 100 percent responsible for my actions and my results.

Michael realized that his own expectation of being a leader who everyone liked was unrealistic. As president, he needed to learn how to have honest, difficult conversations with people in a way that could benefit them. With his coach, he began mastering this art and then together they thought through strategies to resolve the trust issues in his senior executive team.

First, there was a burning issue with a very talented but culturally incompatible team member. Michael was the only one who believed this woman was capable of becoming a team player, and his stand in the matter was affecting the dynamics of the executive group. With his coach, he designed a strategy for her development that included executive coaching and a ten-day expedition to Antarctica to do environmental cleanup. After navigating foreign oceans and working and living with a group of international executives along with an explorer, this senior executive came back from the extremely harsh polar environment a changed person.

Second, Michael had assumed that part of his role as president was to solve internal team conflicts, so he had established a pattern of being the go-between for his senior executives. Michael and his coach decided to put the entire senior executive team through a trust workshop to disrupt this pattern and start to develop new habits. They designed the session around the team members being honest about who they didn't trust and then having conversations directly with each other to restore or re-create their relationships. Everyone benefited from learning how to have honest conversations and the team's performance improved tenfold. Afterward, several people approached Michael expressing their desire for him to stop holding back, to have difficult conversations with them, to challenge them to grow.

"Working with a coach made me a different person. I'm much more confident in my abilities and my contribution. I take more ownership. I believe in myself and my ideas. Coaching made me a leader people were looking for."

Michael Rosen

Michael's work with his coach not only helped him respond more powerfully to his challenges, but also transformed who he was being as a leader.

Under Michael's leadership, the Background Screening Division successfully established a global presence and grew 12 to 20 percent annually. One last expectation remained to be tested: an assumption that the company's new CEO would continue to invest in this successful business unit and take care of what Michael had spent fifteen years developing. But that was not to be. After the new CEO dismantled Michael's team and sold the business, Michael did what he does so well: he co-founded and began leading ProviderTrust Inc., a new health-care risk mitigation and technology services firm based in Nashville, Tennessee.

My conversation with Michael leaves me with two strong

impressions. First, our results are directly connected to our ability to respond. And second, the scope of the responsibilities we assume is limited only by the trust we have in ourselves and our ability to keep holding the tension between our vision and our current reality.

REFLECTING

"You can't coach someone who's not responsible."

Dr. Marc Cooper

This phrase has haunted me ever since Dr. Cooper spoke it in his interview. At first I thought, of course. Someone who doesn't want to take responsibility for their life will probably either not want to be coached or will resist it at some point.

We all have commitments and obligations to fulfill, but that doesn't necessarily mean we *will be* responsible for all of them. If we don't genuinely want to be responsible for something, we won't be. But now I'm realizing that there's more to this issue of responsibility. Many of the coaches I'm interviewing talk about it in the same way my coach does.

"When you realize you are responsible, that you are able to respond to everything (as we all are), you're no longer a victim. When you get that, then it's all about responding powerfully."

Tim Seeton

These coaches speak of drawing attention to the instant between something happening and our responding to it—to that (sometimes all too brief!) moment when we can choose in the gap between stimulus and response. That doesn't mean they join us "on the court" and make our choices for us. It does mean they will be responsible for holding us in high regard and simultaneously helping us develop our competency at responding powerfully to whatever life throws our way. Our responsibility in all this: to get the most out of their coaching.

Great coaches assume responsibility for holding us in unconditional positive regard. This was the one thing almost every coach I interviewed shared with me. Many spoke of "loving" their clients—not in terms of romance or eros, but in terms of agape. Selfless, unconditional positive regard marked by nonjudgmental care and compassion. Being held in the coaching space in this way allows us to increase our self-awareness and be with our discomfort, to respect ourselves, and to learn how to become more effective at being responsible for what we care about.

"Coaching is an improvisation between two people. It is about the dance, the experience you co-create. There is an energetic flow often taking place between the words—within the pauses of a coaching session—where the real wisdom and learning lies. Trust is essential to the process. As a coach, I hold my clients as creative, resourceful, and whole. They know, internally, what the next step is for them. It's my job to create the container for that wisdom—and the essential beauty of their humanity—to emerge."

Jill Van Note, JVN Coaching

"Love and a real deep compassion and care for another human being are essential for a successful coaching relationship. Everybody needs somebody to believe in them. To be a positive light for others, to be a successful coach, you have to have the utmost respect and love for human beings."

James R. Garn, Prosper, Inc.

"I need to love them as who they are before I take them on."

Anabella Shaked

"The coach ultimately loves his players. Ultimately that's the key to the relationship. You've got to love your player. Even if they're really not fun to love. You don't have to like them. But you've gotta love them. That's the key."

Dr. Marc Cooper

"Love is the essence of coaching. By love, I don't mean feeling. Love is giving space for the other person to be the way they are. I tend to relate to people as possibilities. I view them as bigger than they see themselves, and my job is to have them see themselves through my eyes so they see how magnificent they are."

Jim Selman, Paracomm International

"The context for my clients: I just love them. If you can't find a way to really authentically love your client, you really should not be coaching them."

Dr. Joan Bragar, Boston Center for Leadership Development

"One of my most important responsibilities as a coach is to love that person, no matter how they show up. Not in the romantic Hollywood version or the 'you gotta love that car' sense. But from a place of compassion and acceptance of what it means to be human."

Kim Loop

"I love people. They are puzzles to me in terms of how they think. Which is exciting to discover. I'm honored to be in their presence. I give them dignity to exist."

Marcia Martin

"Breaking through has to do with how the person doing the coaching is being. There are hundreds of ways to coach: what really matters is why you're doing it. If you're not doing it in the service of bringing peace and compassion to humankind, you're doing it to make a buck or look good or help somebody make more soap. You have to look at the true motive or vision of the person doing the coaching as they live their life—not what they say. Are they kind and compassionate? *The only thing that makes the difference is whether or not the coach has unqualified positive regard for the person they're talking to. That is what transforms.*"

Charles E. Smith

Effective coaches make a point of staying off our court so that we can focus on mastering our game. Being held in such positive regard, coachees often inadvertently invite their coaches onto the court with them. There's a fine line here. In most cases, it's important that coaches respect and empower their coachees as players by letting them be responsible for their own performance on the court. Coaches decline the invite to play and maintain integrity as "coach": they communicate, show up, remain accessible to their client, but they stay out of the game.

In some cases, it may be appropriate for the coach to consciously step in as an "expert" and provide specific services for a predetermined period of time to forward the action. For example, an executive coach can deliver workshops to team members, like Michael's coach did, without getting pulled into organizational politics. However, it's important to note that the system *will* attempt to recruit the coach into the game—especially when the coach has industry-specific experience or expertise.

> "When I first started coaching out of manufacturing, my most difficult clients were in manufacturing. I was constantly getting pulled into their manufacturing issues. I could feel the pull to share my ideas, my solutions to take their pain away. The great challenge now is to express to clients that I do not necessarily need to be an expert in their industry. Of course, clients do want to know you have some sensitivity to the environment they work in. It's a valid concern, but overemphasized."

> Mark Cappellino

Obviously, shifting from the sidelines to the court can deliver critical value to clients. If done repeatedly, however, the coachee may start to lean into their coach. The coach needs to pay careful attention to what's happening in the relationship to continue to be responsible for the coachee's development towards delivering their intended results.

> "Every once in a while I find an exceptional relationship where they come to trust me so much that they'll just do what I say. When I get to that point, I'm very responsible for what I say."

> Charles E. Smith

No matter what the situation, it's in the best interests of the coachee to continue to be responsible for their actions and to not expect the coach to carry the ball for them.

Successful coachees are responsible for getting the most they can out of their coaching. Coachees who assume that gaining insights marks the end of the process miss the full potential of coaching. Unfortunately, some people are addicted to not being in action. Like dilettantes and workshop groupies, they fascinate themselves with acquiring knowledge. The full promise of coaching can only be realized, however, when we take action toward fulfilling our vision. The steps may be incremental. The journey may be slow and long. But when we're in action, a new synergy can start to develop between coach and coachee.

> "Sometimes I cannot intellectually explain where things come from. There's something in the synergy between us. It creates this third mind: the coachee's mind, the coach's mind, and this third mind of us together. I can't explain why that happens, except that it is a function of the type of relationship we're in: deeply committed, deeply collaborative, a lot of caring, and very high levels of trust."
>
> Val Williams, Influential Presence, LLC

Extraordinary coaching relationships are a collaborative dance, a synergistic co-creation. Coach and coachee tap into a field of collective wisdom where new perspectives, unforeseen possibilities, and innovative actions just appear. Coaches can sense this synergistic connection when it starts to happen, as well as the vital energy it generates. It's like the fire-in-the-belly rush that flows between a high-performance athlete and their audience.

> "An elite athlete who has developed beyond ego recognizes that the energy from the audience is not a one-way thing: the athlete can bring it to their performance and then cycle it back out. Same with the coach. It takes practice to get that cycle going, and it requires the coach to form a container for the

relationship to increase the likelihood of co-creative success between the coach and client."

Ryan Leech

Great coaches have mastered how to be comfortable in this fantastic space and how to maintain a sense of equanimity when they're uncertain where things are going. They have your endgame in mind, they may have a rough game plan in some areas, but they're willing to just show up, be present, and see where things want to go in the conversation. They'll pay attention to and follow hunches. They'll be curious to explore pathways that open up with you. And they'll be willing to share their observations about where things end up when a co-creative coaching conversation concludes.

INTEGRATING

This brings me back to my (perhaps unreasonable) choice to be 100 percent responsible for all my relationships. I would like to bring the synergistic flow that happens in my coaching conversations to all my friends, family, and colleagues—to my whole life in fact. For when I'm talking with my coach, life becomes simpler and saner.

I try working with this for a while.

I can't quite seem to get to serenity. I find myself falling short on the 100 percent, and then beating myself up for not being in integrity all the time. For a while, I hesitate to go further with my coaching. A niggle intrudes: a sense that perhaps I've missed working on the one relationship most critical to my success. My relationship with myself.

What might transforming this relationship make possible?

DISCOVER

Now is the time.

You've established a safe space with your coach.

It's time to do the inner work—whatever that may entail. It's time to release any ideas you may have about the "rightness" or "wrongness" of your path. Time to persevere in removing whatever blocks you from resolving your dilemmas, dealing with your crises and transitions, realizing your highest purpose.

Watch as your coach shines a light on your potentiality.

You have given them permission to awaken you to the unique expression of the collection of atoms and molecules that is "you." Allow them to call forth your greatness, your courage, your compassion. Receive the full extent of their contributions to you. And let them be kindled by the fire of your growth to go further in their own development.

Your coach will walk with you for as long as you wish…until the end of your shared journey.

BEING

I'm seeing a direct connection between who I am being and my results. The through line starts with me and ends with the outcomes of my actions. In between lies an ocean of perceptions and relationships and choices.

My new focus on responsibility and integrity—on speaking my "truth"—has me wondering again about who I am. I'm not looking at my business card, my driver's license, or my tax return to find answers. This isn't about roles or statistical data or income. I ask my coach to hold up a mirror and help me see myself clearly. I want to see who I am through his eyes. The mirror he holds up is one simple statement:

"You are your commitments."

I live with this thought for a while. A quick scan of the obvious commitments I've made at work and in my relationships reveals nothing new. Longing for wisdom, I take a deeper dive into my values, searching for what's important to me. Briefly surfacing for air, I dive again into my not-so-obvious commitments and the beliefs that continuously undermine my confidence.

The image of a subtle blue pearl of light comes to me in my dreams. I remember my friend Michael sharing with me that this symbolizes potential, the source of creativity, the generative power of our spirit, our inner essence.[2]

I contemplate the organic process that produces a pearl. It seems much like the method I unconsciously used as a child to protect my heart. When anything got under my skin, I would grow a defensive layer of stories and beliefs around the irritant to protect myself from further harm, hurt, and disappointment. Over time, I became attached to this accumulation of thoughts, my worldview. Unfortunately, my commitment to being safe hardened into a shell inside of which I am now afraid to be myself.

The blue pearl hauntingly calls me to abandon my familiar defenses, to have faith that I am enough, and to believe that I'll be able to respond to whatever comes my way.

It's time to live from my heart.

MEETING JOHN

Strange that I've never seen this filter of my worldview—or its limiting influence on my life—until now. My curiosity about other people's perspectives on coaching overrides my anxiety to please. I'm actually looking forward to my next conversation, to discovering the worldview of a dentist and in what ways coaching may have influenced his business and his life.

> Dr. John C. Lo starts by telling me he couldn't figure out why he had been unsuccessful in working with a management consultant to improve his five-year-young dental practice. That is, until he began working with a coach who specialized in solo practice dentists.
>
> The consultant had focused on fixing problems for John by providing different matrices and programs for him to use. Dr. Lo made his way through the business tools, but didn't see the results he needed. For example, he had attempted to train his staff on how their phone conversations should proceed with patients. He had handed them a prepared script, assuming they wouldn't understand or do it unless he told them how. This cookie-cutter approach had come across as a commercial: clients could tell these conversations weren't genuine expressions of a personal commitment to them or the practice.

We're constantly bombarded by communications, so much so that we can almost immediately sense whether or not someone genuinely cares about our well-being. All the more reason to simply be ourselves.

The first thing John's coach did was orient him towards working on the person responsible for the practice's results: John.

"The thing that threw me at first when I started talking with my coach was that all he was working on was me. And at first, that's extremely uncomfortable. When colleagues have asked me about working with him, I tell them it's great if you're prepared to look in the mirror. But you have to be prepared to look."

Dr. John C. Lo, Dentist/Business Owner,

Lo Family Dentistry

In coaching conversations, John was invited to take a different approach: to start with exploring his own commitments and clarifying his business goals. For him, commitment showed up as understanding what inspired him, what he really believed his values to be, and what drove him. John took what he discovered in these areas, noted what his goals were, and began to work with his coach to design his practice around who he was—and not who he thought he had to be or what others thought he should accomplish.

"There is no recipe, as much as I wanted there to be. Self-help books are about how to fix your life with this program. There's value there, but people really need to take the next step. They need to make it their own."

Dr. John C. Lo

As John talks, I realize the coaching conversations I've been in recently about my business haven't been about creating infrastructure or processes. They've focused on my fear of being authentic and of "taking the stage" as myself. Abandoning the approval-seeking character I've been playing all these years could give me the freedom to choose what I want, rather than what I think others want me to choose. That has me listening differently to people around me.

John looked at the people he had working with him and assessed whether their values aligned with his own. He began to believe that his interest in creating relationships with his patients as human beings, rather than seeing them as a set of symptoms, could shape his practice. He listened to his staff carefully to hear who really enjoyed helping other people, who demonstrated emotional intelligence, who naturally generated conversations that built relationships with clients. Seeing that his office manager's innate talents in these areas could create a stronger, more relationship-driven practice, John decided to structure the company's operations around himself and her.

He moved anyone with the attitude of a gatekeeper away from the front desk, and brought in a woman with a natural talent for remembering everyone by name and what they had talked about the last time they were in. Flexible and creative, she had the ability to figure out exactly what to say whenever scheduling breakdowns occurred and to come up with solutions that made patients feel cared for. With two highly committed and aligned people at the core of the practice and an exceptionally customer-focused agent at the front desk, things started to shift.

There's that through line again: the alignment between the future we're committed to, who we are, and what we do. While my inner critic quickly throws a doubt into the mix about my ability to establish that alignment for myself, I hear John hesitate.

"I don't know if I was really prepared or understood what it meant to be committed. It took my coach to help me understand that. I actually enjoy the thought that you can be personally responsible for your life."

Dr. John C. Lo

I hear something reassuring in John's perspective: the idea that joy can replace my anxiety around being responsible. At the end of the day, I cannot fail at being myself: I already am. And I am not failing at being "response-able" for my life: I am already responding to life to the best of my abilities. I relax into listening again.

As John became more comfortable with living his values, he realized that he didn't have to conform to other people's expectations and definitions of success. Nor did they have to conform to his personal philosophy. An opportunity to put this concept of choice to the test soon arose.

Previously, John would have walked a tightrope between taking a hard-line approach and keeping the peace in the business. But when it became apparent that one of his staff was no longer a fit and that she wasn't really committed to the practice values, they mutually acknowledged it wasn't really working and there was nothing wrong with having different operating principles. They chose to go their separate ways—respecting each other's perspective.

"I've really determined what I truly value and who I am. That has become the prism through which I look at things and that defines who fits and who doesn't. It takes time to figure that out, but once you do, things become very clear."

Dr. John C. Lo

Dr. Lo's experience of coaching as a journey towards self-mastery sounds similar to mine. Considering he's further along his path than I am, I'm eager to hear what else he's willing to share.

For the past five years, John and his coach have been accountable to each other: John to his coach for his commitments, and his coach to John for John's performance. That is, if John doesn't achieve his intended results, then his coach is not getting his job done. The combination of being accountable to his coach and of having his coach being accountable for his performance works. The initial business goals John had set, which he had laid out in a

PowerPoint® and then put aside and forgotten, have long since been exceeded. He's realized that coaching is more about the process, not the destination. So John has applied coaching to other areas of his life.

As a parent, he talks with his nine- and twelve-year-old children about being themselves. Choosing to be a father and a friend to his son and daughter, John respects and appreciates who they are, while clearly communicating expectations and providing structures within which they can express themselves as part of a family. When a drama happens at school, he discusses with them how they want to deal with the situation, how to look at it without laying blame or finding fault, and who they really want to hang out with.

As a coach to his son's baseball team, John is committed to creating a culture that encourages each child to be their best. Instead of focusing everyone's attention exclusively on the scoreboard and on defeating other teams, he helped the team win their league title last year by listening to each player, trying to understand where they're coming from, and then speaking in a way that made them feel comfortable enough to explore their potential and play their best.

Dr. Lo doesn't hesitate to share that coaching has positively affected his life and the lives of those around him. He looks to his new running coach for a similar relationship based on fabulous listening, valuable feedback, and shared commitment. And, although he's now comfortable in his own skin and where he is in life right now, he's excited to be living the process of becoming himself and to keep exploring what's possible until the very end.

John's willingness to continue looking in the mirror—even though he's already achieved his original goals with his coach—encourages me to stay on my own path. After speaking with him and with my coach, I know without a doubt that our future is not written in stone.

The good news: we are the authors of our lives. And we can rewrite our story whenever we want.

REFLECTING

Our sense of self is an ever-changing storyline, a framework for making sense of our experiences. Yet, the way we view ourselves may be distorted, invalid, inaccurate, or detrimental. Coaching can enhance our self-awareness and help us learn how to become masterful authors and players.

We're not talking about earning merit badges for our egos here. We're talking about working towards self-mastery: separating our reputation—our identity—from who we are, and seeing what, if anything, is interfering with our ability to generate results. Truly great coaches, already on this path towards self-mastery, can act as our guide.

Great coaches model authenticity, integrity, and self-mastery. By virtue of their own journey, they'll have the ability to stand in our shoes and to see our reality clearly. They'll have developed their intuition, their own understanding of what it is to be human, and can sense our hidden motivations and unexpressed concerns. They'll also have some knowledge of the larger social, cultural, and economic forces impacting us.

They'll be honest about their principles and values, their interests and natural strengths, what they care about. They'll design and live their life around these—without any pretense. They'll have put aside "should" and "have to." They will know how to work with their moods and the moods of others. They'll consistently and fully show up in whatever they're doing. Their very presence will speak of honesty and wholeness.

Effective coaches help us unpack our identity in the world from our true self. We quite often confuse our reputation with who we are. The more established our identity in the world, the more likely we'll want to avoid risking failure. Ironically, the greater our success, the greater the chance we have of losing our connection to that inner spark that brought us to what we're passionate about.

Coaches can support us in separating the story people have about us—our reputation—from our inner essence. They can also help us reconnect and stay connected with our passion, our joy, our true self. Sometimes this comes about by a coach simply asking in the moment what's true for us, and then listening without any interpretation of good/bad, right/wrong, or true/false. Sometimes it requires more indirect or intuitive approaches.

> "Coaching is about seeing with the player's eyes and being able to have the player see what they are blind to that is stopping them from success. To some degree, it does matter that you have some knowledge about the game they're playing so you can speak in the language of that game to be able to coach. But it's really about getting inside the head of the player. I'm able to think the thoughts of the player that they do not say. And being able to do that allows a relationship between the coach and the player that's much more dynamic. I'm able to say to the player what they're already thinking before they say it, or to say it in a way in which the player then goes, 'Wow, this guy really understands!' And in that moment when I speak their thoughts, they open up to a level of trust, affinity, and kinship that allows me to coach them."
>
> Dr. Marc Cooper

Speaking what's true for us—no matter what the situation or who we are with—presents an opportunity to untangle ourselves from our stories and to create an authentic presence. We can develop this "truing" of ourselves as a practice and bring it into all our conversations and relationships.

Effective coaches help us develop an influential presence. This comes from making sure our predominant internal conversations produce our desired outcomes. We don't usually generate the results we want when we're resentful, resigned, or distrustful. That's because people respond to our moods much more than our words. And moods are contagious.

> "It's in their self, in their speaking, in their story, in their way of being. If they haven't been able to shift their way of being in such a way that other people are noticing, whatever results they're getting are usually not sustainable."
>
> Virginia Rhoads

Working with a coach, we can look at our internal dialogue and, if we aren't getting the results we want, we can design a new conversation or a physical practice to shift our predominant mood.

> "Your state of being communicates a lot. A client senses when you're out of alignment, whether they call you on it or not. For example, if a coach is nurturing the development of presence with a client, he must also transmit presence in his state of being."
>
> Ryan Leech

Catching these positive moods and this influential presence from our coach can open us up to seeing a whole new range of possibilities for the future. And then, when we learn how to generate and embody positive moods and presence "on demand" ourselves, we can more effectively enroll others in who we are and what we're up to.

Transformational coaches can focus us on consistently being the person we have chosen to become. When we open up to who they are as a coach, we may have, like Dr. Lo did, the opportunity to one day see ourselves as they see us.

"A great coach communicates to people so that they see themselves in the way the coach sees them."

Tim Seeton

This offers as much of a foundational breakthrough as any other results we might achieve through coaching. Just learning to bring this kind of integrity and honesty to our coaching relationship creates the possibility of a truly transformative coaching engagement. From there, we can "true up" who we are being in every moment with all our conscious and unconscious commitments—and bring our whole life into alignment.

INTEGRATING

Sometimes my coach speaks in laser beams. That phrase, "You are your commitments," has cut me open. Who I am is *not* my identity. My identity, my reputation in the world, reflects the commitments I made in the past and the actions I took based on those commitments.

Who I am, my Being right now, is made of the commitments I'm choosing in this moment. Those commitments shape the future I'm intending to realize.

My coach and I circle back to this relationship between who I am being and time until I really get it. I can consciously change who I am choosing to be in an instant, which will change who I am known to be over time. Assuming that I work consistently with my new practices of mindfulness, responsibility, and risk taking, my actions will be guided by my commitments. Eventually, the word on the street about me will reflect my new identity.

Who I choose to be in this moment will be the source of my new results.

The question now is what commitments respect the essence of the blue pearl called "Shae"?

> Respect yourself and others will respect you.
>
> Confucius[1]

RESPECT

I have to let someone go at work. Some leaders say firing employees is one of the hardest things they've ever had to do. Firing someone who has volunteered to help sell a project that is dear to my heart I find even more challenging. Especially when we both had the best of intentions going in.

Or so I thought. Now I'm not so sure.

I've been listening to excuses for nonperformance from this man, ten years my senior, for several months. All logical, all dealt with by me providing whatever was missing. Long, caring conversations about our different perspectives. Then, when it came time to deliver, an unanticipated attack on me for his lack of results and a lot more excuses for not doing what he said he would do. Plus a blatant attempt to take over leadership of the organization.

How little I've respected myself, my core values of integrity and clarity, in this last while. I've unconsciously allowed this person to drain my energy, my time, my passion for the work. My intuition was shouting out months ago that he wasn't aligned with our culture. Out of respect for him, I refused to listen.

My coach asks me who I want to be in this. My first thought: someone who wields her trusty sword and vanquishes the dragon threatening the kingdom. And then I remember my own experience of being fired and what it felt like being at sword point. Using force in response to hurt is *not* the context in which I want to operate.

My next thought: I want to be a leader who gracefully uses her hidden powers to have a conversation with someone who hasn't acted with integrity. A more mature response requiring some dialogic dancing skills.

A novice at dancing with dragons, I invite my coach, who has abundant skill and experience at leading people, to contribute. He speaks of respect—starting with his respect for who I am, where I am in my life, my unique journey. Then he speaks of respecting myself and my commitments. And then he speaks of respect for this person who is giving me an opportunity to learn a new way of being caring.

I'm still collapsing the idea of caring *for* someone with caring *about* them. My orientation towards caring for others is still intact, as if the adults I interact with are, like my baby sisters once were, not creative and resourceful enough to care for themselves. This disempowers my adult colleagues and leaves me invisible, my needs left to be taken care of last.

I'm not three years old anymore. Neither are they. I'm not interested in having someone I perceive as a saboteur on my team. Without trust and respect in a working relationship, we end up dancing around what's missing and struggling to *make* things work. Just as I danced with my old boss, everything we do gets interpreted inside a context of mistrust. The issues and concerns we raise cannot be heard or addressed.

Today, I'm definitely not interested in controlling or manipulating people to *make* things work.

Today, I'm taking care of myself and the work I care about.

Today, I'm letting someone go—respectfully—out of self-respect.

MEETING RICHARD

Getting a relationship, a project, a team, or an enterprise off the ground takes direction, commitment, and alignment. After letting go of my colleague this morning, I feel like I'm coming back home as I settle in to talk with New York–based Richard Move about his creative work and coaching.

> As a multidisciplinary artist and artistic director of MoveOpolis!, Richard's life and work are inextricably linked. He established his reputation for his performances as Martha Graham, as well as

accumulating notable experience working as a runway model, nightclub impresario, dancer, special events producer, choreographer, filmmaker, and director. Like many whose work is a life of art (and whose life is a work of art), he has a tendency to overcommit himself.

I'm with Richard there. I can easily get caught up in exploring several creative possibilities simultaneously and forget to focus.

Richard wanted to work with a well-trained and experienced coach who had a background in the performing arts on "leveraging his best and ditching the rest." As a TED Fellow,[2] he was offered an opportunity to work with a coach who generated his respect: a woman who knew the business, the challenges, and the commitment required to live an artist's life firsthand, having had a successful career as a performer in New York before playing a leading role in the evolution of the coaching field.

"I didn't know what to expect. What I learned right away is the coaching process needs to be with somebody simpatico. My coach understands the artistic psyche, the mentality, the commitment, the pressures. That was especially beneficial and important to our coaching process. I didn't have to speak with her as if she didn't know what I was going through or talking about."

Richard Move, Move-It Productions

My coach doesn't have a background in the performing arts, but he has an amazing ability to intuit my perspective and understand the world I live in—almost as if he's standing in my shoes, seeing through my eyes. Sometimes he even puts words to what's going on with me that is only at the edge of my awareness.

Richard was juggling multiple commitments when he first began coaching. Besides doing course work for his PhD, he was trying to work on his dissertation on dance, performance and its relationship to new media, while continuing to choreograph, perform, and produce live works for stage and film. Richard's ability to assemble an amazing mix of collaborators—including the likes of Baryshnikov and *Sex and the City* costume designer Patricia Field—to work with him speaks to how well he is respected. While having many opportunities to express yourself through your work may be a blessing in the current economic climate, it can also be a risk for an artist with a reputation for a fascinating present and a limitless future,[3] who has trouble saying "no."

Richard's coach, respectful of his talent and dedication, invited him to create a mind map to look at all his commitments and to consider which ones were fulfilling him and which ones were draining his energy. Seeing how thinly he had spread himself, they agreed to work on what Richard was initially drawn to coaching for: clarifying what he wanted his legacy to be, looking at his current body of work, and then designing his life towards realizing specific long-term goals.

From my perspective, taking time to do this can help us accept and honor what we have created in our lives so far.

Working together via phone, Richard and his West Coast–based coach balanced confidential sharing with respectful objectivity. He felt safe discussing critical decisions with her, including what project offers to accept and whether to continue moving forward with his postgraduate degree while maintaining a professional career. Instead of feeling constantly caught up in the frenzy of the New York scene, Richard was able to step back and create some space to think things through with her in the context of his personal "big picture."

"When you're an artist and it's your life, there can be an emotional, almost therapeutic quality to coaching. I'm certainly close and intimate with my coach. But at the same time, there's enough objectivity that she can help me make some hard decisions that are removed from knee-jerk emotional responses."

Richard Move

During his first ten months of coaching, Richard embarked on a new production of *Martha@…The 1963 Interview* for Dance Theater Workshop. His coach helped him keep the spotlight on the quality of his work, a focus which trickled down into each rehearsal and every interaction he had with the cast, collaborators, production administrators, and theater staff. Richard became more respectful of people's time and energy, including his own. He would enter the rehearsal studio with a specific agenda related to delivering a tour de force performance, and emerge three hours later having completed his mission. He appreciated and worked more compassionately with the vagaries of the dancers' bodies, which can be in great condition one day and exhausted the next. He prepared himself mentally and physically to deliver an extraordinary seventy minutes of uninterrupted "Martha."

Outside the studio, he practiced prioritizing his conversations and e-mails to be as efficient as possible, and came to accept that there will always be something left to do tomorrow. And, resisting the pull to get bogged down in minutiae, he worked with his coach to empower others. Richard's new focus, intense commitment, and willingness to create opportunities for people to make critical contributions to the production became contagious—inspiring everyone to give their best and influencing the show's success.

As a self-confessed perfectionist, I know it's not always easy to balance the drive to perform to our full potential with respecting our humanity. My appreciation for what Richard is up to with his coach grows.

Richard began to relate to his academic studies at New York

University with the same thoughtfulness and respect. Their program, the first in the world to focus on performance as the object of analysis, has been ranked number one among theater and performance studies programs in the US. His coach, who is also completing a postgraduate degree, helped him concentrate his efforts here as well: their conversations clarified the essence of his research, why it was important to complete his dissertation, and how he could manage his time to simultaneously support his scholarly work and his artistic practice.

Richard's fascination with and expertise in the phenomenology of the live body moving through space and its unique relationship to photography and film has broad implications in the field of dance, for dance media is often used in learning repertory and reconstructing old works. Seeing this as an integral part of his legacy, he chose to only take courses and write papers that related to chapters in his upcoming dissertation (instead of studying some of the many diverse and unrelated subjects that interested him).

By keeping his eye on the prize, this fully funded Corrigan Fellow has been able to finish his course work and exams, and now has several years to focus on completing his dissertation. Richard acknowledges the profound influence coaching has had on his life, and he continues to work with his coach on achieving what is most important to him artistically and creatively.

As we wrap up our call, I'm struck by how precise we have been in our conversation, almost as if Richard and I had prearranged our time together to give and get everything we needed from each other in the few minutes we had. I recognize this mutual respect, this high intentionality. It's the same kind of immaculateness my coach and I have created in our relationship.

REFLECTING

Coaching relationships evolve. Like a dance, they move to a rhythm and a flow all their own. The dance may start off relatively smoothly if both partners have simpatico lifestyles or common life experiences. Yet a shared background isn't essential: what matters most is what happens once the music has started. The initial trust granted to each other in the early moments of a coaching relationship, can, like Richard's did, develop into something much more valuable, depending on:

- The extent to which coach and coachee respect each other as human beings and respect each other's choices

- The consistency with which they fulfill their promises to each other

- The stand they are being for each other's success.

Coachees implicitly acknowledge they respect a coach with their request to be coached. Starting out with a background of shared experience and credibility can contribute to quickly establishing mutual respect. We may hold a particular coach in high esteem based on their reputation, accomplishments, talents, abilities, or qualities. Based on their identity in the world, we show them regard and consideration. The backgrounds of Richard and his coach warranted their mutual respect.

Great coaches choose to work with people they respect. It is out of this respect coaches can accept and hold their clients in a context of unconditional positive regard. With this foundation in place, the coachee doesn't have to be a certain way, see things only from a certain perspective, or be made to do something specific to win their coach's approval. Being coached involves being seen, heard, and respected for who we are, as we are. Being coached also includes being trusted to make our own choices.

Respect, like trust, is something we grant others. Yet, it is conditional, often dependent on whether people live up to our expectations. When someone we respect does something we cannot condone, we may withdraw our support and admiration. Respect, like trust, also needs careful tending. In a coaching relationship, respect plays out in the dance of integrity.

Effective coaches make our integrity visible to us. For coachees, being in integrity about the commitments that define our game isn't necessarily easy or intuitive. One can never promise to deliver on a commitment. One can, however, promise to take an action. So being in integrity is about learning how to make a big commitment to do something you don't know how to do, promising to take actions consistent with that commitment, and honoring your promises.

Coaches make our integrity visible to us when we look with them at what actions we're taking and what promises we're keeping. A coach can point out if our actions appear incompatible with what we've said we're committed to, if certain actions are missing, or if we're not in action at all. They can also point out broken promises that may reveal hidden conflicts in values and commitments. Surfacing these and discussing what has us break promises can move us closer to being in integrity faster than policing our every promise.

Richard's intention to "leverage his best and ditch the rest" sparked this kind of integrity check. Being in integrity isn't about doing absolutely everything you say you're going to do. It's about being rigorous with the promises you make and communicating rapidly with the people concerned when breakdowns occur. Aligning our actions with our authentic commitments can help us adjust our course so we're headed in our intended direction.

Effective coaches clearly communicate their standards of integrity to us. Some of the coaches I interviewed will drop a client if they make a promise and don't keep it; others will give their clients three strikes before declaring them out. Still others will work with people to help them master keeping their word.

> "Honoring my word is the field of play for coaching. Ultimately, what determines the outcome is the way someone experiences the way I am being compared to the way they are being."
>
> Charles E. Smith

Some common agreements made between coaches and coachees include: showing up on time, promptly communicating when one can't deliver on a promise, and speaking authentically and courageously about what is and is not working in the coaching relationship.

In a profession based mostly on word-of-mouth referrals, profound integrity counts for coaches as well. Their success as a coach relates to whether their word is good: they need to establish that kind of rapport with their clients to build a reputation. As an expert, their integrity also lies in following professional standards of conduct, referring out anything beyond one's current level of competency, being someone people can trust and count on, and honoring any agreements made with their clients.

In effective coaching, both coach and coachee take responsibility for the integrity of the relationship. Integrity for the coach can also sometimes be about keeping ego off the dance floor. Coaches, like all humans, can fall under the spell of being valued by clients, which can sometimes occur like an ego stroke. Left unchecked, ego can drive the coaching and activate an overemphasis on controlling the process, the person, or the coaching outcomes.

> "So much of coaching is getting yourself out of the way. I can't emphasize that enough. The job of the coach is to stand squarely in the agenda of the person you are coaching, period."
>
> Vince DiBianca

Self-aware coaches will often catch themselves before ego strokes influence thoughts or behaviors. However, both coach and coachee need to remain vigilant about being mutually responsible for sharing what they sense is happening in their relationship. Any hint of being "controlled" or "manipulated" by either person can signal the need for an authentic conversation. For suppressing our natural responses to disrespect and control diminishes our experience of the benefits of coaching.

> "The coach is only as good as the player. When you get the right match, one plus one equals infinity and

beyond. It's this magical thing that happens. When you do the coaching right, do the technique, get your own crap out of the way, when you're both present and the client is willing and able, incredible things happen. It's more than the sum of its parts."

Madeleine Homan Blanchard

Engaging together with a sense of curiosity in an inquiry about what's going on in the relationship opens up the possibility of optimizing the coaching. Sharing what you're both sensing and feeling—without holding it as "the truth"—allows you to sort out what's going on for each of you, to see whether you're projecting something onto the other person, and to sort out what "crap" belongs to each of you that needs to be taken care of and respected. This kind of generative conversation, done well, can enliven rapport and expand the coachee's sense of self-awareness. From here, coach and coachee can focus their time and energy on what's most important to move the coaching forward.

In effective coaching relationships, both parties stand for and honor each other's way of being and success. Mastering the dance steps without engaging in the spirit of the dance won't deliver an extraordinary performance.

Mastering the process of coaching without respecting each other—as we are and as we choose to be—*and* simply engaging in the win/win spirit of the relationship won't deliver breakthrough results. We've already encountered the idea that the coach stands for the coachee's success in whatever they're committed to. Inside that context, the coachee stands for the coach succeeding in that enterprise. As such, they become partners in creating a triple win: success for the coachee, the coach, and the relationship.

INTEGRATING

Being coached has given me a chance to consistently experience profound respect, trust, and integrity in relationship with another human being. I'm consciously aware of noticing, valuing, and embodying these principles in our coaching relationship. Bringing this new way of relating to other relationships in my life seems—at least in theory—as if it will be easy.

In practice, as I start creating some consistency in who I am being in all situations with all people, I notice something strange happening. I still catch myself—and my coach catches me, too—ever so subtly speaking in ways that disparage my character and my competency or acting in ways that ever so slightly insult or show contempt for who I am. This pattern of disrespect reflects a choice I made a long time ago to be disrespectful of myself.

My new commitment to help leaders communicate more effectively to create positive change in the world calls for someone who is a source of confidence, trust, and respect.

What if I am not who I think I am? What if all the internal conversations I have had about myself were thoughts—nothing more—and not the "truth" about me?

What might be possible if I give the gifts of self-respect, self-trust, and self-confidence to myself?

> What separates the men from the boys is how you respond. Boys shut their eyes—they refuse to look into the abyss. The men look. They own up to ambiguity and conflict. They own up to reality.
>
> Daniel Smith[1]

PATTERNS

Now that I've danced with an external dragon, it's time to dance with the last of my internal dragons. The deeply buried patterns of thinking, feeling, and responding that hold me back from expressing myself. The patterns that hold me back from being successful.

I'm afraid to look into this abyss. I tell my coach that it feels as if I'm opening an inner Pandora's box. Just taking the lid off could release untold negative forces that have the ability to destroy me, my life, and others. That's why I put them in the box in the first place.

My coach acknowledges my fear. He points out that I don't really know what's in the box. Right now, I'm predicting that everything I discover will be a threat. I could keep the lid on and continue living as I am. That is one possible future. But perhaps—and a brief smile flashes across his face as he says this—perhaps that is not what's in the box. Perhaps a different future is possible if I take the lid off.

The choice is mine.

A week passes. For seven days I contemplate the gaps between my life now and the life I envision. Seven days I look at my ongoing concerns, my frustrations, my dead zones. I come back to my next coaching session with an awareness that, although I've now fired someone, I still tend to avoid difficult conversations—at work and in my marriage.

My relationship with my husband has been pervading my thinking these days. It feels like we're no longer living into the same future, as if we're growing apart. But I don't know that for sure. I talk about everything *but* our relationship with him—avoiding what I anticipate will be an angry conflict. So we never get to find out if we're aligned or not. We live an uneasy life together.

This holding pattern, this not speaking of the elephant in the room, doesn't work for me anymore. So I ask for coaching on how to have a conversation with my husband about our marriage. My coach works with me to separate facts from feelings, to identify what I want and what I see is missing. He invites me to relate to what's happening as an opening for a breakthrough in my relationship with my husband.

I couldn't foresee that communicating from my heart with my husband would begin a chain reaction of breakthroughs that are still playing out to this day.

MEETING FRANK

I know the focus of my coaching was supposed to be my business, but what's keeping me up at night right now isn't my work. Thinking and rethinking every interaction I have with my husband is interfering with my ability *to* work. I'm grateful to have established enough trust with my coach that I can have this conversation with him. It isn't something I want to talk about with friends or family. There's a subtle pull towards looking good with them that doesn't allow me to share what I'm going through: it would dispel the illusion of me having everything under control and expose them to information that might color their thinking about my husband—and me.

As I hear Frank van Schaayk's assistant transfer my call through to his office, I wonder whether it's really possible to break free of the behavior patterns we establish with the people closest to us—at work and at home. Frank's cheerfulness intrudes into my reverie and within seconds I'm caught up in his story.

In 2012 Frank B. van Schaayk found himself turning to an executive coach for the second time in his life. Seven years earlier, a coach had helped him transition from being an "operator" to becoming CEO of McCain Foods Limited's US business. Back then, his coach had started with a 360-degree assessment and then worked with Frank to co-design a six-month action plan. Implementing that plan helped Frank shift from being an expert in his field to being a true business leader. And now, as Regional President - The Americas, he was turning to an executive coach again. This time, the coaching focus was two-fold: on closing the gap between his intentions and his actions as a senior executive leader and on contributing to a larger transformation initiative for the company.

"I've come to see that the most important thing you can do is observe people in action and listen and look for things that are missing. Look for that gap between intent and action."

Frank B. van Schaayk, Regional President - The Americas, McCain Foods Limited

Frank met his new coach through a strategic planning process organized by the multinational's new CEO. With the world of food changing more rapidly than ever and consumers looking for healthy, sustainably produced food choices, McCain needed to do something different to avoid placement in the past due date category. That "something different" included a powerful journey of self-discovery and transformation for Frank.

Ouch! Past due date category, indeed. That phrase hits home, and I suddenly realize that many of my colleagues and friends are similarly experiencing something unworkable in their work, their health, or their relationships right now. We all have some issue going on that's worth addressing before our expiry date.

Like many business leaders, Frank found himself getting stuck thinking and rethinking how to pursue opportunities while simultaneously trying to solve problems. This high achiever would spend many hours replaying what had happened in a day and reconsidering possible future actions. What he most needed to break this stressful pattern was someone who could effectively disrupt his thinking and then create the space for him to look differently at his circumstances.

"The pursuit of achievement is definitely relegated to quarterly earnings in corporate America. The stress and turnover impact lives. If we could pursue achievement in a more positive sense and create exhilaration from it, just think what this country could do."

Frank B. van Schaayk

We each deal uniquely with challenges and problems. Frank's default behaviors included constantly trying to come up with solutions and directing his displeasure and authority towards making something happen. His normal operating mode created an endless cycle of worry ("Am I coming up with and choosing the best solutions possible?") and frustration ("Am I being who I need to be as a leader?").

I know how hard it can be for us to take effective action and achieve peak performance when we're stressed and anxious. Part of my recent coaching has focused on establishing consistent practices of meditation and exercise that improve my ability to stay relaxed. I wonder where Frank and his coach went with this.

For his own well-being and that of the company, Frank needed to transcend his very human fear of failure. So he turned to his new executive coach to help him learn how to become comfortable with discomfort, how to create new patterns of thinking and acting that would help him be confident that—no matter how tough the situation—he'd be able to figure out a way to make things work.

Frank's coach invited him to first observe whenever he began to feel frustrated and then to interject a new idea into his thinking:

challenges, problems, and failures are essential stepping-stones on the path to success. As he practiced observing his automatic responses and relating to his circumstances from this new perspective, Frank realized that he was creating a powerful opening for positive development and unpredictable success. Viewing events as opportunities—instead of threats—helped him start to shift his automatic responses in stressful situations.

When his son came to him after failing to secure a visa to travel to England for a summer job, Frank chose to see it as an opportunity to share what he had learned. Frank listened to a story of an intelligent, talented engineering and architecture student experiencing several days of frustration trying to find answers in an endless maze of online bureaucracy. They discussed where anger had shut his son down and what he might possibly do next.

After their conversation, Frank's son shared his challenge with his mother, who suggested he contact a firm Frank had used in the past for ideas on how to have passports and visas expedited. One phone call directed the young man to an online process that the firm had created for people trying to get into the UK for similar purposes. Within forty-five minutes, he had an application submitted and an appointment booked. Their shared learning— looking at things from the point of view that "what's happening is a breakdown, and I'm on my way to a breakthrough"—not only reduced stress, but also allowed them to relax and think outside the box.

Being uptight certainly leaves no room for patience, respect, or curiosity. When we're relaxed, we can initiate a respectful dialogue, air our assumptions and ideas, and explore possibilities—without the threat of manipulation or coercion. It sounds as if being relaxed primarily comes from shifting our thinking, not necessarily from shifting how we're using our body (although exercise definitely helps shift *my* mood and tense muscles!).

"I'm more confident, more grounded and balanced,

more constructive. Because I don't have this noise in my head of frustration and anger, I can listen and look for opportunities to pursue or improve. It allows me to provide feedback and to seek feedback, to start a more virtuous cycle of bringing more aspects of myself to my interactions."

Frank B. van Schaayk

Together, Frank and his coach looked at other places where his actions and intentions weren't aligned. One of Frank's executives wanted to be promoted, but Frank couldn't fully get behind that. What he could genuinely commit to was helping the individual be the best executive they could be in the context of the business they were currently running. What was left unspoken in their relationship had been impacting their work together, so Frank had a conversation with the executive to re-create their relationship on the basis of what his real commitment to them was. Over time, Frank worked with his coach's distinctions around commitment and language as a rigorous framework for his leadership and was able to fundamentally change this relationship by behaving and acting consistently with his commitment.

This "truing up" of his commitment respected both Frank and his colleague. It seems that breaking their habitual way of relating moved them beyond a yes/no response to the question of a promotion and brought them instead to what was true for each. Frank's honesty opened the door for them to create a third alternative together—a no *and* yes response—that both could authentically endorse.

Frank saw value in the leadership distinctions he was learning and intended to apply them to an ever-increasing number of daily business situations and challenging circumstances he and his colleagues faced. It just so happened that being authentic about commitments and consistently acting in alignment with those commitments was beginning to play out within the company's global leadership team.

In the past, the team's normal response to a crisis—like the instinctive behavior of many leadership teams facing a threat—had been to have all hands on deck. The executive team would hunker down in a room together with the intent of finding someone to take on the bulk of the responsibility for closing the gap. Failure on a grand scale was a possibility for that chosen leader. Executives would do their best to stay out of the limelight and continue to focus on protecting their silo, their people, their local plans. Frank noticed he—and others—would become a lot less friendly and a lot more stern and curt in these meetings.

Frank's coach was part of a team of senior executive coaches working with the global leadership team on disrupting these patterns. Some of the McCain executives admitted they didn't really believe it was possible to achieve something unprecedented in the company's history. The executive coaches worked with them as a group and as individuals on what it is to commit to something that appears impossible, who they need to be as leaders in relationship to that commitment, and the breakdowns they anticipated encountering along the way to realizing that unprecedented future.

Once the global leadership team aligned around and committed to a shared vision, they began working on what actions they needed to take to produce extraordinary results. Encouraged by the global CEO, their conversations shifted towards winning *together*, instead of just winning. The executive meetings began to focus more and more on creating breakthroughs, inventing what hadn't been done before, strengthening the whole company in terms of practices and processes. Within five months, they increased McCain's global earnings (before interest and taxes) by double digits relative to what they had believed possible.

Their vision has not yet been completely realized, and their work with the team of coaches continues.

Committing to a shared vision creates a context that can pull team members to create new, more collaborative ways of relating. Ways where being *for* each other improves working *with* each other. How I'd love to be able to create that kind of teamwork at home; then, when things break down, we could realign around our commitment to the same vision of the future.

> "There's enormous benefit in understanding who you are and who you're being in circumstances of all types. It goes far beyond business to impact your life in many different ways. I've never been as comfortable with myself and as positive as I am now."
>
> Frank B. van Schaayk

As a leader, Frank is also still working with his coach. He wants to consistently help people see the connections between how they relate to breakdowns and their successes. And he intends to celebrate those successes more.

Recently, his son made him very aware that this is Frank's learning edge—at work and at home. The younger van Schaayk had obtained outstanding marks in all but one subject at the end of his first semester at university. Frank's automatic response was to focus on the lowest mark as a problem to be solved. His son asked if that was really where Frank wanted to go first. Gently laughing at himself, he said, "No." Acknowledging his son's achievements and his courage for calling him on his commitment to celebrate success opened the door to an entirely different father-son conversation.

Frank's conversation with me has affirmed that coaching often spans the artificial boundaries we set between our business, our family, and our well-being. The habit of dividing our life into compartments helps for coordinating and organizing, but not for harnessing change to our advantage. Once we start looking at interrupting our patterns, all domains come into play. Everything is interrelated. And everyone.

We're not the only ones who can benefit from our coaching.

REFLECTING

Our brains are wired to make split-second decisions based on what has worked in the past. Unfortunately, what worked before may interfere with and limit what's possible for us now. We learn how to drive a car and then operate almost on "automatic"—until the day we lose an arm and need to develop a new way to drive. We get married and, over time, start operating on auto pilot—until we realize our patterned ways of communicating don't help us connect with each other anymore. The same happens when we don't produce the results we intended at work and revert to habits that worked in the past.

Working harder and longer based on the same thinking and same actions that got us here only gives us more of the same and reinforces the gap between our intentions and our results. If we relate to the gap as a *problem*, we can end up fixating on achieving results. No matter what we do, we can only expect to produce something incrementally better than what we've already produced. If we don't observe our patterns and then take the time and effort to have those difficult conversations, we end up effectively repeating the past and never resolving our dilemmas. Our old winning strategy becomes a losing strategy.

"In my experience, people want to be coached. People do want to delve into the deeper depths of who they are and how they can be more effective. I think that's natural to us."

Vince DiBianca

Successful coachees choose to relate to the gap between intentions and results as an opportunity to experiment. The most powerful access to success lies in changing the internal conversations we have about ourselves and others, about our circumstances and time. These are the conversations that really drive our choices and actions. Over time, they become habit, a soundtrack stuck on replay. Even when we know this internal tape does us no good, we continue to run it. With a coach, successful coachees become more effective at generating their intended results by using the "gap" to explore new ways of observing, thinking, and responding to the world.

Rather than follow conventional wisdom and try to "break" habits, transformational coaches help us create new ones. Habits are, by definition, sticky and persistent. Coaches interrupt our habitual thinking patterns and invite us to observe our thoughts, moods, and physiological reactions, to use the gap in time to consciously choose between an automatic and a new way of responding. They can support us as we sort out what old tapes to replace and as we begin to design new conversations, habits, and actions that better serve our commitments.

"All the linear assessments of coaching only get to the form. Coaching is elevating the spirit of who you're talking to. The challenge in coaching has to do with what knocks your energy down. How do you recover from that? Coaching is all about recovery. All you need to observe is the energy flows around you. When your energy expands, the world around you improves. All you need to trust is the rise in your own energy and vitality."

Charles E. Smith

Transformational coaches also help us discern the price we pay by running our old tapes in terms of energy, vitality, and results. They can bring a heightened awareness of where we may be hypocritical or unconscious.

Great coaches act as a mirror, reflecting back to us where we may not yet be using all the power, leverage, and influence we have to realize all that's possible. Coaches have committed conversations with us to point out our uncommitted conversations in a compassionate and forceful enough way to get our attention.

"Sometimes the greatest coaching occurs like a whack on the side of the head."

Vince DiBianca

Uncommitted conversations keep us trapped in the past: they fixate on storytelling, complaining, blaming, criticizing, making excuses, protecting ourselves. Committed conversations focus on moving us into action: identifying whatever is inhibiting performance, creating new relationships with people and circumstances, and aligning with ourselves and others on doing whatever needs to be done.

Great coaching delivers a sustainable state change. People often equate the work coaches do with skills development and self-improvement. They anticipate working with a coach will ensure they lose any "bad" habits and acquire the skills they need. And then they'll have more of what they like about themselves and less of what they don't like; they will be "changed." Such a prescriptive approach to coaching can deliver change, but it won't always deliver sustainability. Change alone is second prize.

The grand prize in coaching is sustainable change. Transformation. The profound and continuing shift in our worldview and our way of being that opens up entirely new possibilities to us. The state change that increases our self-awareness, our competencies, and our choices. This kind of shift can have us reexamine our values, our purpose, and our legacy.

"Coaching becomes most powerful when it leads to an authentic transformation. In such an instance, the coach and the person being coached both experience a 'new way of seeing' self, others, challenges, and possibilities. Like achieving balance when riding a bicycle, this new way of seeing doesn't deteriorate with time.

How this transformation comes into being is not well understood. What seems to make it more likely to take place is when both parties commit to devoting some regular time during the coaching sessions to exploring what may not look to be immediately applicable, but which is subjectively compelling. When this commitment is made with sincerity and backed by discipline, what has been observed is a lessening of tension to deliver hard results and the spontaneous emergence of core values that often include treating people with dignity and compassion—without sacrificing performance standards. What emerges is highly creative and practical problem solving, along with an authentic concern for the greater good beyond commercial success."

Dave Laveman, Laveman & Associates

Transformation can reorient us from being disempowered—at the effect of the past, our stories about ourselves and other people, and our current situation—towards being the author of our life.

"Transformation isn't about fixing or changing. It's about creating a new state of being—like the state change from water to ice. You can skate on ice, but you can't swim in a frozen pond. The most potent shift in being that occurs is the shift from being at effect of life (being a victim) to being 'sourceful' in the face of circumstances (being an author/leader). Successful people are powerful in the face of any circumstance, including the most dire and seemingly limiting ones— they turn breakdowns into breakthroughs and tragedies into triumphs."

Vince DiBianca

Transformational coaching is at the heart of extraordinarily effective coaching. It's a different dance than what many people are used to. It's not a dance everyone wants—or needs—to do. We can certainly receive coaching to improve our skills and competencies without setting foot here. However, we will likely want to engage a new worldview or way of being with the guidance of a coach when we're trying to successfully navigate crises, transitions, or dilemmas.

And if we want to experience life in a context of self-expression, joy, and fulfillment, then we'll want to work with a coach who's prepared to dance this way with us. Someone who, at the end of our time together, will leave us standing on our own two feet, comfortable with discomfort, fully responsible, authentic in our integrity, and accountable for our commitments.

INTEGRATING

I'm seeing that it is possible to break free of my old patterns. I'm also seeing that how I do one aspect of my life is how I do all my life.

Creating new habits of thinking and acting inside the context of my coaching relationship is having a spillover effect. I'm trusting myself to communicate from my heart more consistently in my relationships with spouse, family, friends, and colleagues, even in situations where I feel someone else is holding all the cards. I'm changing the conversations I have with myself and with others. I'm respecting others by not trying to fix or manipulate their responses. I'm resisting the urge to try to solve their problems. I'm paying attention to what they're committed to and to my energy levels when I'm with them.

I wonder where this will lead.

"Clients think they're going to hire a coach and they're going to be so smart and they're going to tell me what to do and they're going to have all the answers. Like it's going to be a silver bullet and solve all their problems. Well, it is a silver bullet. It does solve a lot of problems. But it just doesn't work the way people think it works."

Madeleine Homan Blanchard

ACCOUNTABILITY

Change the conversations you're having and you change what's possible.

I've been divorced for several years now. Chosen a new career direction, moved, resumed singing, started a new life and a new relationship. But the last few weeks have been more than I can bear. Everything related to my business seems to be falling apart at once. I'm terrified that I won't be able to make this work. I've been having fleeting thoughts of suicide—an experience very foreign to me.

So I call on my coach and tell him I don't intend to take action on these thoughts. But I do want to be *in action* in response to what's happening.

He immediately connects with the difficulties I'm going through and empathizes with me as a human being. He tells me that dealing with suicidal thoughts isn't something coachable: it is something I need to bring to a psychologist or a psychiatrist. However, as my friend and coach, he offers to talk with me about where I am in this moment. I accept.

Thankfully, he doesn't try to convince me that things are better than I think they are, nor does he focus on taking apart my past or my story about why things are hopeless. He doesn't talk to me about my mood or how I'm feeling. Instead, he reminds me of two things.

First, suicide is a choice. And a choice is really an expression of my commitments. If I ever get serious about choosing suicide, he tells me I should immediately call on professional psychological help.

Second, we revisit our conversations about what coaching is. Coaching is about *using* difficulties and circumstances that aren't working as an opportunity to *accomplish* something and to *break out* of the struggle we're in.

He asks me to take a moment to reflect on what I would want to accomplish if I weren't feeling depressed. In the ensuing silence, I realize that I've given up on my game. As we continue talking, I start to acknowledge what's been happening and to distinguish my life as possibility from the tar pit of depression into which I've drifted. The black suffering starts to lift as I reconnect with my vision, the future, and my capacity to commit and to choose.

At the end of our conversation, my coach strongly recommends that I tell this story to a psychologist and spend some time checking out that aspect of myself—separate from coaching. A psychologist can help me in ways a coach cannot. They can look at what from my past is determining my current mood and internal states and, ultimately, driving my behavior.

After our call, I move into action. I talk with a therapist. I declare that I'm taking responsibility for being the source of my own happiness. I ditch unnecessary complications from my past that clutter my living space, like the moth hole–filled blanket my father had given me for my hope chest more than thirty-five years ago. I fly to San Francisco to visit friends and ask them to connect me with people in their networks.

My conversations shift naturally towards who I am, what people are up to, what's needed, where I could contribute. My mood lifts in the sunshine, buoyed on the gentle waves of outdoor saltwater pools and in the presence of new colleagues. I find serenity speaking with an elder and strolling in the mountains outside of Santa Cruz.

I begin a gratitude journal. Starting with a few simple joys, expanding each day to include new ideas, fresh perspectives, and basic insights into the benefits of life that I've not acknowledged before.

In our next call, my coach gifts me with his wisdom around creating opportunities. And then another colleague coincidentally shares an insight about men that alters my entire way of relating to them. This, combined with my new-found wisdom about opportunities, shifts everything. The overwhelming sense of effort and struggle that has been weighing me down for the last while fully dissipates.

I return home with an appreciation of how blessed I am and an awareness that what's holding me back are the stories I've made up about how terrible my life is and how I'm not enough. It's all made up. And I made it up, a whole Pandora's box full of stories.

I empty the box in silence. At the bottom lie the gifts of self-trust, courage, and compassion. Whatever happens now, there's no need to conform or to please anyone else anymore.

I am worthy of having my life work.

I hold myself to account for the promises I keep, the actions I take, who I choose to be, and whatever I have and whatever I don't have in my life. I trust my ability to create my life. And no matter what challenges I may face or how many times I fail, I can keep on creating my life until I succeed.

I haven't solved all my problems.

But now I'm free.

MEETING MARK

Free—and living with a new inquiry regarding my work. Who do I want to be accountable to and for what? That question points to the heart of my business and the heart of my identity. I put aside the answers that immediately come to mind, old ideas shaped by who I saw myself as years ago. The answers I need will come from a new vision of my future and from conversations in my present. Perhaps clarity may even come through my next conversation.

In 2002 Mark Zesbaugh was promoted from CFO to CEO of Allianz. His leadership had been instrumental in helping Life USA, one of Allianz's more recent acquisitions, move from start-up to become the fastest growing life insurance operation in North America. And now he was assuming accountability for the performance of an international financial services company that offered insurance, asset management, and banking solutions to customers worldwide. Mark, seeing a direct correlation between how a company's senior leaders interact and bottom-line results, soon began looking for a coaching firm to help him enhance the performance of Allianz Life's leaders as a team.

Mark looked for people he could trust, people with credibility. He engaged an organization specializing in commitment-based management whose coaches have international experience, excel in athletics, and hold graduate degrees from top-tier institutions. As part of the engagement, the firm's founder, an executive coach, entrepreneur, and former rugby player, took on working with Mark and the members of Allianz's senior leadership team.

"I'm not a big believer in having consultants tell you how to run the company. That's my job. He was able to provide tools to help us communicate more effectively, build trust, eliminate some of the things that were detrimental to the team."

Mark Zesbaugh, CEO & President, Security Life, and
Former CEO, Allianz

Allianz's senior leaders, including Mark, began by looking together with their executive coach at the attributes of an effective, cohesive, high-performance team: trust, communication, commitment, loyalty.

Initial self-assessments in these areas ranked low, revealing a high incidence of unnecessary bureaucracy and triangulation. Having already proved themselves as individual high performers, Mark now held them accountable for their effectiveness as a team and for eliminating the inefficiencies normally associated with a big company.

The idea of holding senior leaders accountable for their effectiveness *as a team* should come as no surprise, but somehow it alerts me to the fact that we're not talking business as usual here. That focus in accountability shifts everyone's attention from optimizing individual performance to optimizing team interactions.

The senior leadership team's coach next gave them consistent terminology for describing some of their behaviors. He coached them in developing powerful new habits of communicating that allowed them to speak directly to each other, openly share their negative assessments, and ask for what was really needed to deliver on their commitments.

As the company's senior leaders gained competency in providing assessments, giving authentic feedback to each other without worrying about repercussions, and making requests, Mark observed a simultaneous improvement in their ability to effectively deliver results. With each request, there was a clear customer and a clear performer. Both parties held each other accountable for the satisfactory fulfillment of the request: the performer for performing and the customer for speaking up about any misunderstandings or gaps. Mark saw that as the senior leadership team communicated more effectively and were seen to be moving in tandem, their new way of interacting began to permeate the organization. The whole company's performance improved.

"One of the things I've always been big on is accountability. People who are performers love to be held accountable. They love to be measured because they want to win. I talk about the thrill of accountability. It's just a matter of following up on commitments. You can still be very specific with what you're expecting. I'm constantly holding people accountable. And they love it. It's not necessarily a bad thing: it's a good thing."

Mark Zesbaugh

This is the first time I've ever heard "thrill" and "accountability" used in the same sentence. The passion I hear in Mark's voice sparks a desire to figure out for whom and for what I'd put my neck on the line.

> Meanwhile, Mark began working with his coach on improving his performance as leader of the team and the company. Mark was certain his coach's commitments were, first and foremost, to his personal development as CEO and, secondarily, to the team's development. He knew his coach was assuming accountability for Mark's results: their unwritten understanding was "performance first, pay later." And he valued what his coach was bringing to the table as an executive accountable for leading his own organization to success. Their relationship rested on a strong foundation of trust and credibility.

Mark's coach assumed accountability for Mark's results. Mark assumed accountability for the company's results. The leadership team assumed accountability for their effectiveness and for removing organizational inefficiencies. Mark is counting on his coach and his team, and the organization is counting on Mark to deliver. Everyone has something at stake in the game. All are playing on the same side; all are playing to win.

> As CEO, Mark was "always on," even when he wasn't speaking. His coach introduced two key ideas to Mark and his team. One, mood is the culture of an organization, and two, mood is not everything—it is the *only* thing. Ultimately, no matter how good your product or service is, if the people in the organization don't have the right mood, success will elude you. Already nimble and decisive, Mark recognized this was an area of his leadership he could develop and leverage. So he began mastering the communication tools and leadership concepts his coach gave him towards being a leader who positively influences the mood of his organization.

> "What's the definition of a good leader? It's not in the eyes of the leader. If somebody gets up and says they're

the best leader in the world, they're probably not. But if their employees get up and say this is the best person I've ever worked for, that's the definition of a leader."

Mark Zesbaugh

To model authenticity, Mark focused on consistently matching his actions with his words. He worked with his coach to fine-tune his self-awareness, his presence, and his ability to confront difficult situations objectively. He made a commitment to his coach to deliver on what he said he would when he said he would. His coach regularly followed up and held him accountable for delivering on his promises to the extent that Mark knew that if he didn't fulfill a commitment, his coach would have fired him and forfeited his own payment. Nonperformance was unacceptable to Mark and his coach.

Having spoken with Mark's coach, I know Mark isn't exaggerating about the level of confidence and commitment in their partnership. I can think of nothing that compares to such rigor in a relationship.

This impeccable approach to authenticity extended to clearly living the values, vision, and goals of the company every day. Mark went through a process with his senior leaders to develop a consistent view of how their executive meetings should be handled: everyone present and participating in the business at hand. Late arrivals and in-meeting texting became history. He ensured that the tough conversations necessary for running a successful business happened in the room, and that when everyone left, they were one seamless team. This had a tremendous ripple effect: having an aligned executive team promoted greater productivity and a stronger culture.

"My coach didn't tell me what I wanted to hear. He told me stuff I didn't really want to hear. Too often as the CEO you're always hearing what people want you to hear—not what you should hear. If I hadn't seen results, I wouldn't have continued."

Focusing on communications, authenticity, and accountability paid off. When Mark left the company in 2007, he had overseen Allianz's annual premiums grow from $3 billion to $14 billion, operating profits increase sixfold, and invested assets rise to more than $70 billion. Allianz Life is now one of the leading life insurance providers in North America.

Mark has gone on to start his own strategic advisory firm and a Bermuda-based reinsurer with other senior industry executives. As CEO of Security Life Insurance Company of America, he consciously communicates what people are a part of, where they're going, and what's expected of them. As well as bringing to his daily interactions the communication tools and leadership concepts he mastered while working with his coach, Mark also brings a sense that he, as leader, should be a coach as well.

"There's something to be said for being proactive, for seeking out a coach you can count on to produce transformative results for yourself and your team early in your leadership," I hear myself thinking as Mark rings off. In this case, coaching helped transform the prevailing habits of a high-performing CEO and his leadership team into more effective ways of operating that provided a win/win for all involved and helped the company significantly improve their bottom-line results. I'm left with a strong impression that taking on coaching seriously *before* you hit a wall, have a major crisis, or move into survival mode can shift your trajectory just as effectively as taking it on in the midst of turmoil.

REFLECTING

Yet, we often don't take on coaching seriously until we do hit a wall. I know that, given the opportunity, I used to opt for lazy. I counted on life to drift along pretty much as it always had and to deliver to me what I already had received (or a little better).

"In the world we live in today, incrementalism is your enemy. This entire process will be a waste of your time and your company's resources if you do not have something of importance at stake in the game."

Chris Majer

In incremental mode, I'll look to make small changes and expect incremental improvements. But to make the most of my coaching investment, I committed to generate breakdowns and then, with my coach, to learn how to use them as openings for breakthroughs. In this alchemical work of transforming breakdowns into breakthroughs, we rely on ourselves and on our coach to bring a few key ingredients to the mix.

Successful coachees place themselves sufficiently at stake in their game. Without a commitment to something of significance to us, coaching will lack the power and potency to generate breakthroughs. Playing for no or low stakes is like trying to have sex with one foot on the floor. An entertaining pastime for some, an exercise in frustration for those who really want to play life full-out.

Successful coachees demonstrate fierce courage. Given the choice between accepting the status quo and going for what's unreasonable, many of us opt to go with the flow and expect life will work out somehow. It often takes courage to face the facts of our lives. When life isn't "fair," audaciously moving into action based on what we *want* to see, rather than what *is*, demonstrates the kind of unreasonable determination that makes us the hero of our own story.

It takes courage to be coached, especially when what we hope to realize seems unrealistic. We demonstrate our courage when we let go of what once served us, try new ways of thinking and acting, develop new skills and competencies, embody new distinctions, and master new practices. It takes courage to stick with coaching through the tough times, when change is jarring, our defense mechanisms are constantly triggered, and we want to hang on for dear life to what we have, and through the boring times, when our work seems to plateau and nothing seems to be happening. It takes fierce courage to be held to account for our promises by someone who is genuinely committed to our success.

Successful coachees are consistently accountable to themselves and their coach. We are the source of our success. We need to be able to count on ourselves to get the help we need when we need it and to find out whatever we don't yet know that we need to know to succeed. We need to count on ourselves to honor our word: to do what we say we will do and to come clean with ourselves and those involved as soon as we know we won't. And we need to be accountable to our coaches for staying in communication, for being fully present, for addressing any broken promises and breaches of trust in the coaching relationship. For when we let our coach down, we let ourselves down.

Successful coachees demonstrate patience and persistence.
With new distinctions from our coach, we can observe the world and ourselves differently. Although nothing changes *in the world*, our fresh perspective makes the world, ourselves, our future appear different to us.

> "The future changes every time you look at it, because you've looked at it with whatever you're looking from right now."
>
> Charles E. Smith

Coaches provide iterative feedback so we can master observing ourselves in action, rigorously examining our thinking and our moods, and discerning what improves our performance and what doesn't. Each time we take in their feedback or shift perspective, the world appears different again. And each "different" can be somewhat disconcerting until we get centered in it with the help of our coach, one reason which is partly why coaching takes time and perseverance.

Great coaches don't let coachees get away with mediocrity.
They go into the game with us as if we've already won. They trust us, yet they'll also verify that we're doing what we say we'll do. They have compassion and unconditional positive regard for us, but they won't let us get away with things.

"I learned a good lesson from my dad about accountability. I went on a date when I was sixteen. My dad told me I had to be home by 12:00, and if I wasn't that I wouldn't get the car that weekend. I came in late at 1:30. I sneak in my bedroom, and start to climb under the covers. And there was my dad sleeping in my bed. What in the world am I going to do? I said, 'Dad, I'm home.' He's like, 'Randy what time is it?' He said, 'What time are you supposed to be home?' I told him, 'You told me to be home at 12:00.' He just said, 'Randy, you're not getting the car this weekend. I just want you to know I love you. Now get under the covers.' I learned that lesson. What he taught me was he loved me, but he wasn't going to let me get away with it either. Coming back to my coaching, when I ask somebody to do something, I expect excellence and greatness from them."

James R. Garn

Like Randy's father, coaches expect excellence and stand for nothing less.

Effective coaches stand in the "inspired certainty" that we _are_ successful. Coaches can give us that push we need when we're stuck. Yet, they hold us as masters of our own fate. They see us as sufficient, capable, and resourceful. They share their belief in us when we have lost touch with believing in ourselves.

"I stand in the 'inspired certainty'* that they can produce anything they want to produce. If they're accountable for what they say they'll do and I'm accountable for what I say I'll do, they can produce anything they want to produce."

Jennifer Cohen (* Attributed to Arjuna Ardagh)

Coaches help us hold ourselves accountable for our results. Effective coaches will not be swayed by excuses, negative moods, or any story we concoct about how things aren't the way we want and why that makes things difficult or impossible for us. They'll keep us present to our own power to create ourselves and our life.

"One of the challenges in a coaching relationship is that people try to enroll me in their resignation or in how tough something is or in why things can't be different than they are. On the one hand, I want to feel what they feel, so I get it. But if I buy their story and sign up for their assessments, I'm no good to them. The best I can be is a confidante or a 'commiserator' or a hand-holder. Empathy is critical—but not sufficient—for powerful coaching. Circumstances are what they are. There is very little that we can control there.

However, I don't see how you interpret circumstances as fixed. You can choose what meaning you give to things, what story you 'live in.' That's where our power is as human beings. I don't ever see you as stuck."

Don Arnoudse

Great coaches genuinely believe in us. When we combine our own fierce courage with the inspired certainty of our coach, we have the makings of a powerful collaborative partnership. But the most valuable secret ingredient of great coaching magically appears in the moments when we doubt ourselves. It is the faith our coach has in us and the confidence they exude that we can be counted on to succeed.

"About three years after I started working in Egypt, one of the doctors I was working with there came up to me and said, 'I want to thank you so much for the difference you've made.' I said, 'You're welcome, but could you please tell me what I did?' He thought for a minute, and then he looked at me and said, 'You believed in us.'"

INTEGRATING

I didn't know what the implications would be of telling my coach I wasn't going for incremental improvement. I had no idea he understood that to mean we were going for transforming who I'm being as I go about doing whatever's required to have what I want in my life. I had no idea what transformation was or what breakdowns awaited me.

I have no regrets.

How big a game we want to play and how rigorously and authentically we want to play it is always up to us.

I've learned that we don't have control over life. I've learned that I can count on myself to deal with whatever life throws my way, and that includes calling on others for help. I've learned that my breakdowns *can* produce breakthroughs. My ego will raise its "little voice" inside my head anytime it feels threatened, but I am not my ego. And holding myself to account for delivering on my promises— to myself and to others—gives my life integrity and makes me more intentional about how I use my time and energy.

Coincidentally, I'm experiencing less stress, less frustration, more serenity, more relaxing into life.

I feel like I'm finally getting out of my own way.

Now where and who will I contribute to?

> "Your personal capacity has to stay ahead of your professional growth. You have to get out of your own way and be courageous enough to share your gifts with the world."
>
> Lisa Nichols,[1] author of *No Matter What*

POWER

Someone mentioned in passing a while ago that my name in Hebrew means "gift." Unbeknownst to them, ever since I went to San Francisco, I've been seriously wondering who to share that gift with. It's only recently that this dilemma crashed in my door and demanded resolution. And by crashing, I mean literally hitting the driver's door of my car.

Only a few weeks earlier, I had been wishing I was dead. Now I'm grateful to walk away from this accident without broken limbs or missing parts. I feel compelled to take immediate action towards living the life I want—and to not settle for less.

I've been in an exclusive relationship for over two years now with a man who lives in another country. We're not getting any younger. I'm ready to make a commitment and design our future together. The only way I can see for us to be with each other in the way that I want—fully empowered individuals coming together as collaborative life partners—is if we marry. Yet my fear of rejection has had me stuck, unable to speak or act with any sense of integrity. My coach responds to my request for a brief impromptu call. In the context of our ongoing work on integrity and responsibility, he makes time to help me articulate what I really want and what that could mean in terms of actions.

So I propose to the man I love—the man I want to share the "gift" of myself with—the day after the accident. Surprised, he acknowledges my courage in asking and says he'll get back to me with his answer soon.

Ten days later, he calls me back. A definitive, unequivocal "No." Along with all the thoughts and reasoning behind his response, what he would be willing to commit to, and a list of the dates he'd be available to hear what I choose to do next. I acknowledge his honesty and declare with even more clarity what I want. Not a ring on my finger, but a live-with intimate partner who chooses to commit to co-creating a future with me. His rejection of my proposal stands.

It's been three months since the accident. Three months of letting go of fantasy. This "no" has been staring me in the face for a long while. Time now to peel back the layers with my coach to see what's true for me and to acknowledge that I have no control over what's true for someone else. Time now to accept the consequences of my pattern of approval seeking and doing whatever it takes to make someone love me. Time to appreciate that asking for what I want and dealing with this "no" completes the transformation that began with my thoughts of suicide.

As I work with my physiotherapist on healing soft tissues and establishing healthy postural and movement habits, I look at what's missing to have the kind of relationship I say I want.

I remember a sign my coach used to have on his desk: "from wanting to get to willing to have." I used to think this reminder was about being intentional and surrendering to receive what life gives us. For a while, I thought it was perhaps also about letting go of being afraid of getting what we want. But I'm seeing something else there now that connects intention with power.

That something is commitment.

Half-assed commitments deliver half-assed results. It's as if half-assed commitments have a half-life. They lack the energy of a full connection with our intention and our power. Eventually, they succumb to exponential decay.

I also know that how I do one aspect of my life is how I do my whole life.

My fear of rejection has been realized again. But this time, I'm standing tall, spine realigned, fully aware of the choices I have in this moment.

I can wallow in sadness, grief, and anger. I can go for the drama of contemplating ending it all. I can run out and find another partner to play the victim game with. I can bury myself in work and let my fear of the responsibility of an intimate partnership with another human being define my future.

Or I can apply everything I've learned from my coach to what's happened.

I've always wanted to stand in my own power. And here I am, devoid of illusions. I'm letting go of what I've always longed for because now I know what's more important: loving myself as I am and being ready to contribute to the world without needing approval and acknowledgment. Perhaps from here, one day, I can create an authentic relationship with a man who loves me as I am—without me having to do anything to earn that love.

I'm choosing to keep being brutally honest with myself about what I *truly* want. And then to *totally* commit to whatever that is.

I'm going to play full-out in all areas of my life *in spite of my fears about committing.*

MEETING LESLIE

I look back on the last few weeks with surprising equanimity. The image comes back to me of Denise climbing a rock wall and learning that she doesn't really know what her limits are. As I prepare to talk with another powerful and successful woman, I wonder what other connections, what other commonalities in our coaching journeys remain to be discovered.

> Leslie McCuaig, international consultant and senior manager of a nonprofit, was looking to make a career change. Her work in the field of international development involved extensive global travel. Having just adopted a newborn boy, she wanted to design her work life closer to her Vermont home. A career counselor

referred Leslie to a female executive coach in the area to find out more about how she was successfully combining local, national, and international work in her business. The two women connected, and shortly afterwards Leslie accepted a generous offer to participate in a private week-long leadership workshop that this executive coach was leading.

The week was transformative for Leslie. Not only did she learn some of the distinctions of leadership this coach worked with, but she also had a breakthrough in terms of how she related to other people—both personally and professionally. During the workshop, she began to inquire into an unresolved tension in an important personal and professional friendship.

While working in Europe the previous year in a high-pressure situation, one of her male colleagues behaved in a way that she disliked. She interpreted his behavior as controlling and didn't hesitate to share her assessment as if it were the "truth" about him. This put a strain not only on their relationship, but also on her relationship with another mutual colleague, Leslie's best friend, who eventually married the man.

The executive coach invited Leslie to consider that we are constantly making assessments, both positive and negative. But our assessments are not truth; they're just our perspective, our interpretation about what happened. Leslie realized she didn't have to throw out the baby with the bathwater. She forgave this man for his behavior and acknowledged his strengths and talents to her best friend.

"I think it's a privilege to be coached. Not everybody gets a coach. If you're a tennis player, you don't get a coach until you're a certain level. It's the stars who get coaches, not the club players."

Leslie McCuaig, Resident Country Director - Moldova,
Millennium Challenge Corporation (MCC)

Leslie pauses for a moment, and I reflect on how I had jumped to interpreting the rejection of my marriage proposal as a rejection of me. Of how I had acted as if that were the truth and judged the man I love, cutting off communication and declaring that I didn't see the possibility of *any* relationship in the future. He had only turned down one way of being in relationship. Now I wonder if I've done irreparable harm and needlessly thrown away "my baby" with my bathwater. Leslie starts to speak again.

> Freeing herself to not have to judge others for their behavior stood Leslie in good stead when she accepted a new position some years later with the Millennium Challenge Corporation, a US foreign aid agency. She called on the executive coach for help in adjusting to her new circumstances. She wanted to have an impact on reducing global poverty while working inside a government context, but she found it challenging to be herself, a rebel by nature, inside the culture of this then seven-year-old agency.

> Her coach was there for her, working organically and consistently with Leslie to create a way of operating inside this new environment that could help her achieve the results she intended. Leslie wanted her coach to challenge her most closely held convictions, to share her wisdom gained from experience, and to give intelligent, honest feedback. Leslie wasn't paying to have someone flatter and agree with her so she could go and do whatever she was planning to do anyway. She trusted her coach to look at things differently, to take her out of her comfort zone, to speak directly, but to really be on her side. So, with this level of trust as the foundation of their relationship, they worked together on how Leslie could contribute the best of her inner "rebel"— her innate ability to be original, bold, decisive, and inspiring—to the noble purpose everyone at MCC shared.

My coach similarly accepts me as I am and grants me space to become whoever I choose to become. He points out when I'm relating to stories, opinions, and interpretations as if they're facts. He doesn't let me get away with coasting. He challenges and champions.

He models what it is to realize one's potential by contributing the best of who he is as a coach to me.

> For Leslie, contributing her best meant letting go of some of her preconceived notions about what was possible inside a government culture. Being diplomatic, for example, doesn't preclude being unreasonable or direct. Leslie surprised her coach by making an unreasonable request for the sake of the whole organization. She wanted to share a huge opportunity to address a genuine organizational need with all of MCC's resident country directors at their annual conference in Washington, DC. The conference organizer listened to her pitch and offered an hour on the last day of the event. Leslie, remembering her coach's words ("If you're trying to do something bold and extraordinary, make unreasonable requests..."), responded with a request for a three-hour slot to lead off the first day. And she got it.

> She was ready to move to her next level of leadership.

> Move she did. She turned with a new enthusiasm to her position leading a country office in Moldova for MCC, where she had recently moved with her two young children, finding herself for the first time on the inside of an embassy community. Her main responsibility was supporting and overseeing a newly established quasi-governmental project management group, led and staffed by highly qualified Moldovan leaders and experts.

"If you're taking on new challenges and new situations, if you're lucky enough to get somebody to coach you, it helps you grow more. And everything's more fun when you're growing more."

Leslie McCuaig

Challenging circumstances and new situations used to have me always feeling "less than"—a mood that people picked up on and that left them doubting my competency. But these days, my little interior litany of, "You're less effective, less confident, less intelligent, less able to respond, less successful than you could be here," is fading into memory. Now, my self-doubt has been replaced with the wise words of my coach. More and more, I can be present in a conversation, objectively observing what's happening, listening for what I can contribute, and making big offers and requests. But I'm not entirely consistent with this: I can still get knocked sideways by my own anxiety, anguish, or inauthenticity and end up feeling like an outsider rather than a player.

At first, Leslie saw herself as an outsider in Moldova. Fascinated with learning how things worked in this foreign country, she watched and listened to what had happened, what was happening, and what wasn't happening. All the while she felt she was without much influence to transform what she was observing: local politics, strong personalities, and already existing bureaucracy that functioned between the local implementing group and the MCC in Washington. Yet, she was there to help these people use the MCC grant funding to formulate their own practical, innovative, and flexible solutions to the problems they faced—without running afoul of two government bureaucracies. And one of the most critical necessities to succeed was a committed leader contributing to having their organization function really well.

Leslie's coach challenged her to put a stake in the ground and be that leader.

Leslie accepted the challenge.

"She was a cheerleader, trying to get me to own and exert my power, my intelligence. If anything, I'm probably getting more open with her as it becomes less important to assert that I know what I'm doing and more important to be aware of what I could be doing better."

Leslie McCuaig

First, she needed to identify where she had the right to assert herself in her position and where she didn't. From past successes with similar projects, Leslie knew she excelled in situations where she was responsible for generating the vision. But here there was no vision. And no results, yet. There was only an expectation that the vision be created and owned by the people in the organization. So she initiated an inclusive, collaborative process to generate a vision that the thirty people in this organization could own and get behind. She brought her executive coach, who is also an expert in organizational transformation, to Europe to facilitate this work.

As Leslie talks, I see her demonstrating a competency I haven't fully developed yet: enrolling others in collaborative partnerships. I see the impact of this in the two places in my life where I want to generate this kind of relationship—with my life partner and in my business. My anxiety about proving myself tends to have me trying to force my solution to a problem on others. This drowns out the possibility of me hearing what's *really* needed and wanted. I fixate on selling the solution and what I can give you, and miss the opportunity for partnership. Yet, how much impact can we really have if we're not listening for each other's concerns, expectations, and limitations, if we're not being open to what we each can bring to the relationship and what we both care about?

Leslie wondered what impact she might be able to have when she wasn't choosing the direction or the destination they were moving toward. Through conversations with her coach, she gradually realized that she would add value to the project by contributing her unique perspective to the work they were doing together and by continuing to use all her skills as a leader and manager. Her responsibilities wouldn't end once the vision was clear: she also needed to continue to develop and lead people in action. Navigating everyone through the envisioning process and all the things that were going to happen afterwards, regardless of where they chose to go, was where she could make a difference.

While this envisioning work was underway, Leslie began to see that she also needed to accept her role in the embassy community in which she and her children were living. As one of the highest-ranking individuals in the community, she couldn't take a back seat. So she embraced being a leader there as well. Rather than resisting the differences between life in the private sector and life in government, she found herself accepting the support of others and appreciating what that support provided her family. Just being a leader in this very different group of people strengthened her own sense of self.

When we embrace our power in one context, we can avail ourselves of it in others. Perhaps part of being successful in life includes bringing our whole self to all environments and all situations.

Back at work, Leslie wanted to exercise her power with humanity. Bureaucracies tend to perpetuate the command-and-control style of leadership. Leslie, profoundly moved by her breakthrough around judgments and forgiveness, chose to relate to her colleagues as human beings. Perfect in their imperfection and worthy of compassion.

Leslie worked with her coach on developing her capacity to consciously create openings for people to respond authentically—even (and especially) in moments of pushback or conflict. For her, compassion shows up in moments when it's not easy to be present with another person, when it's not easy to give them the space and permission to be whoever they are choosing to be. And when they choose to behave in ways that aren't aligned with their commitments or shared vision, Leslie chooses to neither write them off right away, nor get triggered to respond emotionally to their actions.

Within her community and her organization, Leslie receives many compliments on her leadership. She is known as "the calm one," the one who doesn't take things personally. The woman who leads with humor and grace, even when everyone may be trying to influence her to control others, she wisely operates from the premise that *she* is the only person she can control. And she has learned a vital lesson from her coach.

Being empowered makes a difference.

"One of the things about coaching is you're never done being coached. You're never in a position where you won't do better by being coached."

Leslie McCuaig

REFLECTING

Every coaching journey is unique. Some last months, others, years. Some leave us with new skills and abilities, others with an entirely new way of observing and being in the world. Sometimes we aim for change, sometimes transformation.

No matter what the focus or duration, effective coaching moves us in the direction of feeling better, doing better, living better. Going the distance together—however long it takes, however much we learn and shift, and wherever we end up—is a privilege. And a shared responsibility.

Successful coachees access the full potential of the coaching relationship by being responsible and unreasonable. They are responsible in looking to see what's needed. They are unreasonable in taking it on fully—without holding back and without relating to either who they are now or their circumstances as limitations.

Once they've identified what in-the-world outcomes they want to realize, they work with their coach to continuously generate a dance towards getting those results. It's not a performance one can predefine. It's a back-and-forth, in-the-moment co-creation. And the dance goes only as far as the coachees are willing to take it.

"What makes for an extraordinary coaching relationship is the depths the client will go to in order to change. When they're willing to really look at themselves and how they have their life set up, when they're willing to question how they've been operating for a long time because they see something's not quite working, when they're willing to go to that depth and be that vulnerable and open to questioning things they've held pretty sacred, and then they will explore another viewpoint and we do it together. When we find a new place and they shift into it and they can be more successful, that I find extraordinary—especially when I could not have predicted it. Because we're truly creating something together. That's when it's *truly* extraordinary—when it's a surprise like that."

Val Williams

Coachees who choose to go for transformation engage in the work of the courageous. Transformational coaching can be a collaborative partnership to uncover what's already there—you, your potential, your greatness, your spirit—and to realize unprecedented outcomes that will be the fullest expression of your soul at this time. This is the work of the courageous.

Transformational coaching evokes our whole self to be fully engaged in the moment, in life. It connects us with our power—our capacity to create, to do and accomplish things, to act effectively. Transformational coaching connects us with the intangible that shapes the tangible, the spirit that is at the center of all. In the eyes of a transformational coach, we can see the reflection of the blue pearl of our soul. And, if we look at them with the same unconditional positive regard they show for us, we may see their soul as well.

Great coaches, like great leaders, use power—not force. They allow people to be as they are and as they choose to become. They powerfully interact with them on the basis of their commitments. They leave people at choice: present to their ability to choose in the moment.

"What I'm really after is choice and freedom. This is the true purpose of the life of the coach."

Charles E. Smith

Great coaches aim to see their coachees walk away one day, empowered, strong, able, and capable of performing effectively. They know that any dependency on their coaching runs counter to the original agreement with their client.

"I'm coaching people to find their power, their voice, their truth, their authenticity, and to free themselves up."

Leslie Tucker

Once we emancipate the power we already are through coaching, we can produce as if by magic.

Great coaches know when it's time to let go and allow their client to be on their own. Although we all can benefit from coaching throughout our lives, when the coaching relationship has been set up with a clear endgame in mind, the approach of the ending will be obvious to both people. If the relationship needs to conclude before the endgame happens, it is often because this was not the right goal, the right relationship, or the right time to move forward together. Whether or not the endgame has been played, both coachee and coach will need and want to reflect on the effectiveness of their work together.

In many cases, the coach initiates and the coachee drives this dialogue. Whether the conclusion happens when an artistic production closes, when a coaching contract ends, or sometime before the coachee has fully achieved the results they set out to realize, clarity and objectivity need to remain in the forefront of the conversation. Coachee and coach can share with each other their observations, acknowledgments, and assessments of whether the coaching has been effective—always remembering that the coachee owns their results.

"My ultimate goal as a coach is that they're moving so quickly towards what they want that I can't keep up with them. They're done. They're generative and they've put enough shape around their challenge or opportunity. They've hit their stride and they're on their way. And now it's just a matter of wrapping up the relationship for now and leaving them alone so they can do their work."

Kim Loop

Ideally, these assessments will be grounded with evidence of the quantitative and qualitative results that have been realized. When the endgame has been played, one can include any number of observable outcomes in this evaluation: rave reviews of a performance, demonstrated proficiency with new competencies, promotions and successful presentations, along with intangibles like decreased stress and frustration, increased self-confidence and ease. If the endgame has not yet been realized, sharing observations about what has worked, what hasn't, what has been learned, and what remains to be addressed can be valuable for both coachee and coach. Having a conversation to complete the coaching and the relationship—whether the journey together has been long or short—offers both people an opportunity to say what needs to be said so that they are free to move forward without any unfinished business.

Those who have been blessed to experience transformation through a truly collaborative partnership with their coach will know that this extraordinary relationship never really ends.

The wisdom, love, and spirit of a great transformational coach remain with us, until the end of our days.

INTEGRATING

My coach and I have declared our work together at this time is complete. We agree that I can call on him, when and if I need his perspective in the future. My gift to him in this last session is to tell him what his coaching has made possible.

Clarity is often a function of contrast. So I compare my life at the beginning of this process to my life now and share the unexpected outcomes of our coaching relationship that I hadn't foreseen.

Before I began coaching, I was a like a sleeping beauty, unconscious of who I was and sleepwalking towards some vague idea of what might be possible for me. Today I am awake and more fully accessing my creativity, talents, and power to generate my life.

I've realized that who I am is just a story—a story I made up and which I can rewrite any time I choose. Whatever I'm doing in this moment is an expression of whatever story I'm playing out.

I'm responsible not only for my story, but also for my relationship to myself. I'm responsible for my life. I'm responsible for what I create.

I've let go of the idea that I can be everything to everyone, let alone be everything to someone. I am choosing to be a creative, compassionate leader. I am choosing to be a woman who trusts herself to be fully self-expressed. A woman who is compassionate with herself when she forgets who she is. A woman who is compassionate with others when they forget who they are. I've taken the lid off and my whole life is now a resource for exercising this leadership.

There is no need to prove myself. There is no need to save others. I am enough and they are enough. I trust myself enough to step out into the world and listen for where I'm needed and wanted and what I can contribute.

I've chosen to live by seven principles that emerged from my experience of being coached:

1. Listen generously.
2. Be fully present and authentic in my speaking.
3. Care about the people I'm talking with.
4. Hold people in unconditional positive regard.
5. Build trust.

6. Be courageous.

7. Be committed to helping others get to choice.

I've incorporated coaching into how I work with clients and reoriented my business to serve coaches, leadership development consultants, and leaders. The more I share my values and commitments, the more people are attracted to me who share those values and commitments. The more vulnerable I am in sharing myself, the more people see me as courageous. The more I respect other people's perspectives, the more trust we build. The more I open my heart, the more connected I am to others. And more and more resonant opportunities keep showing up for me to share my gifts—and to receive gifts of friendship, financial remuneration, and ongoing learning.

I've let go of the idea that there is an absolute "Truth," even the idea that I may have access to a "truth" that is constant and irrefutable. Truth varies from person to person. What is "true" for one person is not true for another; truth lies in the eye of the beholder.

My current truth is that coaching has shifted my experience of life. I can still be afraid, but now I trust life and accept what is happening, rather than trying to force things to happen in a specific way or manipulating people to respond in ways that are not true for them. I intentionally create all my relationships—with myself, others, my circumstances, my life. I am no longer being a victim in my story.

I am the fantastic space in which my life occurs. I am no longer being a victim of the circumstances of my life.

This aliveness I feel now—this "being well being human"—is success.

I'm at home everywhere.

Thanks, Coach.

"Transformation is ultimately a spiritual phenomenon.
Spirit is at the heart of effective coaching.
And as soon as you start talking about it, it's not there."

Charles E. Smith

We become the stories we tell ourselves.
Our future depends on the stories we believe today.

EPILOGUE

Does the story you're living into end in success?

That's up to you.

Does the story we're living into end in success?

That's up to us.

For our stories—like our conversations and our lives—weave together in ways we cannot predict. Our conversations, the ones we have with ourselves and the ones we have with each other, determine the future. We co-create the world we live in with the choices you make, the choices I make, and the choices we make together.

The breakdowns we are experiencing today are complex, interrelated, and persistent. We are being called to come together across boundaries of politics, economics, and culture to create new possibilities at all levels of society—from our families and local communities to our countries and the world. We are being called to create shared contexts—fantastic spaces—that will allow us to collaborate effectively to take on the challenges we face together. We are being called to look at reality from all kinds of different perspectives and to effectively engage in creating positive, sustainable change.

"We have a lot of problems in our industries, in our world, that aren't for single minds: they're for team minds. These aren't solved by one person waking up one day and saying, 'What if they did this?' It's solved by teams of people working in that Wikipedia model— on the court, in the field, or in a boardroom. It happens with multiple individuals working together."

Jonathan Young, Digital Marketing Senior Manager,
Life Technologies

We already have a common way of looking at what different perspectives make possible. We have a common way of relating to each other that builds mutual trust and respect across time and space, that allows for honesty and constructive criticism, and that can turn our most promising ideas into reality. We have a way to create sufficient foundations of relationship to make the difficult choices that must be made and to do what needs to be done.

That way is the way of coaching.

The masterful coach's way of being can be embodied and brought to bear in every part of our society and in our daily lives.

"I'm being the coach. I see the world from a coach position. I live into the world to inspire and draw forth and bring forward that potential and have people be better off—in their own assessment—than they felt they were before they met me. It's bigger than 'Are you a coach?' and 'Do you have clients who have asked you to coach them?' Are you *being a coach*? And how is that showing up in the world? That's one of the gifts the industry brings to the world. More and more, we're creating that paradigm in which people look to see how can I inspire, how can I contribute, how can I see what's possible—rather than what's *not* possible. To have that viewpoint is a real asset now. We're in a big moment of having it be sustainable or not and having people be connected or not. It's a powerful conversation to be in."

Marcia Martin

I believe it's possible to do what's never been done before. And I believe what's at the heart of effective coaching relationships is being—and can be—applied much more broadly in the world.

It's when the odds seem against us that great coaching, great leadership, and great collaboration show up. Whether we're coaching our child's baseball team, leading a company, or collaborating virtually with people from around the world, we can "true" ourselves to the common threads of coaching outlined in this book.

I'm not suggesting that anyone who is up to making their life work or the world work *has* to go out and hire a coach in order to be successful. I *am* suggesting that we can learn from great coaching relationships and great coaches.

We can experience what it is to be truly present with another human being, fully committed to their success and to our success. We can discover the lasting rewards of an empowering collaborative partnership.

Answers are our past.
Possibilities are our future.
Choice is our present.

ACKNOWLEDGMENTS

It takes a team to write a book. I am forever grateful to all the people who helped *The Blue Pearl* happen.

To all the extraordinary players who shared their experience of coaching with me, thank you for the contributions you make in the world. Without your belief in your coaches, we would never have met.

To all the great coaches from around the world who agreed to be interviewed for this book, thank you for sharing your perspectives, stories, and time with us. Without your belief in the value and potential of coaching, this book would not exist.

To all the people—past and present—who coached me and have been coached by me, thank you for the opportunity to learn and grow together. Without your contributions to my life, I would not be who I am today.

To Jim Selman, thank you for being my coach, my mentor, and my friend.

To Rick Fullerton, thank you for inspiring me to write this book and for being my guide in the second year of its creation.

To Matt King, Chris Creamer, and Dr. Marc Cooper, thank you for your unfailing support, feedback, and encouragement during the research and writing of the first draft of this book.

To Olivia McIvor and Leslie Eveland, thank you for your friendship and for our long creative conversations, without which I would still be doing interviews.

To Bruce Preville, thank you for consistently speaking to the author and the leader in me.

To Charles Berkstresser and Laurie Varga, thank you for your expert creative guidance in the final stages of the production of this book.

And to Paula Sarson, thank you for helping make my writing sing.

APPENDIX
COACHES INTERVIEWED

Although not all coaches I interviewed have been quoted directly in this book, I would like to express my profound appreciation and gratitude for the contributions everyone listed here has made to my understanding of the "common threads" in effective coaching relationships.

Don Arnoudse
The Arnoudse Group LLC
www.arnoudse.com

David Boothroyd
University of British Columbia Opera Ensemble

Dr. Joan Bragar
Boston Center for Leadership Development
www.bostonleadership.com

Mark Cappellino
Primary Leadership LLC
www.markcappellino.com

Jennifer Cohen
Seven Stones Leadership Group LLC
www.sevenstonesleadership.com

Dr. Marc Cooper
The Mastery Company
www.masterycompany.com

Vince DiBianca
Praemia Group LLC
www.praemiagroup.com

Dr. Mary Edwards
Coaching for Artists & Creative Entrepreneurs
www.coachingforartists.com

Renee Freedman
The Freedman Collaboration Group

Dr. Rick Fullerton
Fullerton Consulting

James R. Garn
Prosper, Inc.
www.prospering.com

Nancy Miriam Hawley
Enlignment, Inc.
www.enlignment.com

Allan Henderson
GHJ Consulting

Dr. Carolyn Hendrickson
Tandem Group, Inc.
www.tandemgroupinc.com

Alexandria Hilton, MCC
EUROUS Global Executive Leadership Inc.
www.eurous-global.net

Madeleine Homan Blanchard, MCC
Blanchard Certified
www.mhblanchard.com
www.blanchardcertified.com
www.coaching.com

Anton Lahnston
Lahnston Associates LLC

Gina LaRoche
Seven Stones Leadership Group LLC
www.sevenstonesleadership.com

Dave Laveman
Laveman & Associates

Kevin Lawrence
SGI Synergy Group Inc.
www.coachkevin.com

Ryan Leech
www.ryanleech.com

Kim Loop
Human Systems Renewal

Chris Majer
Human Potential Project
www.humanpotentialproject.com

Marcia Martin
MM Productions
www.marciamartin.com

Michael McDermott
Arcadia Group
www.arcadiagroupus.com

Anne Miller
A Miller & Associates LLC
www.annemiller.net

Mary J. Murphy, CPCC
Global Conversations
www.globalconversations.ca

Dr. Madi Navon
Geneva Consulting
www.madinavon.com

Virginia Rhoads
Jempe Center
www.jempecenter.com

Kay Sandberg
Global Force for Healing
www.globalforceforhealing.org

Jim Selman
Paracomm International
www.paracomm.com

Tim Seeton
Paracomm International
www.paracomm.com

Anabella Shaked, MA MCC
The Adler Institute, Israel
www.anabella-sh.com

Charles E. Smith
Kairos Productions Inc.
www.navigatingfromthefuture.com

Leslie Tucker
Roundstone International, Inc.
www.roundstoneintl.com

Jill Van Note, PCC
JVN Coaching

Maggie Weiss
Sage Alliance Partners
www.sageap.com

Val Williams, MCC
Influential Presence, LLC
www.valwilliams.com

NOTES

Desire

1. Confucius, BrainyQuote.com, Xplore Inc., 2013. http://www.brainyquote.com/quotes/quotes/c/confucius11927 5.html, accessed June 10, 2013.

Dilemmas

1. Brian Herbert & Kevin J. Anderson, *Dune: The Machine Crusade* (New York: Tor® Tom Doherty Associate Books, 2004), page 120.

Transitions

1. Benjamin Disraeli, Goodreads Inc., 2013. http://www.goodreads.com/author/quotes/47030.Benjamin_Di sraeli, accessed June 10, 2013.

Self-Improvement

1. John Wooden & Steve Jamison, *Wooden on Leadership: How to Create a Winning Organization* (New York: McGraw-Hill, 2005), page 34.

Learning

1. Lawrence Pearsall Jacks, *Education through Recreation* (Harper & Brothers, 1932), page 1.

Assumptions & Expectations

1. Carl Jung, Goodreads Inc., 2013. http://www.goodreads.com/quotes/630036-your-vision-will-become-clear-only-when-you-look-into, accessed June 10, 2013.

Competency

1. *COC Magazine*, April 1988 in Maria Corvin and Betty Nygaard King, "Judith Forst," *The Canadian Encyclopedia* (including *The Encyclopedias of Music in Canada*) (Historica Foundation, 2012).

http://www.thecanadianencyclopedia.com/articles/emc/judith-forst, accessed June 10, 2013.

Commitments

1. Michael Ray, *The Highest Goal: The Secret that Sustains You in Every Moment* (San Francisco: Berrett-Koehler Publishers, Inc., 2004), page 23.

2. Will Ferrell and Adam McKay, *Anchorman: The Legend of Ron Burgundy* (DreamWorks SKG, Apatow Productions, and Herzog-Cowen Entertainment, 2004).

Discomfort

1. Napoleon Hill, BrainyQuote.com, Xplore Inc., 2013. http://www.brainyquote.com/quotes/quotes/n/napoleonhi4017 11.html, accessed June 10, 2013.

Being

1. Hillary Clinton, BrainyQuote.com, 2013. http://www.brainyquote.com/quotes/authors/h/hillary_clinton _4.html, accessed July 15, 2013 AND

   People magazine, Time Inc., April 29, 2010. http://www.people.com/people/package/gallery/0,,20364464_2 0365309_20777461,00.html, accessed July 15, 2013.

2. Michael L. Ray, Chapter 2 - The Blue Pearl, "Two Questions", unpublished manuscript, 2003.

Respect

1. Confucius, *Sayings of Confucius*, Goodreads Inc., 2013. http://www.goodreads.com/quotes/184307-respect-yourself-and-others-will-respect-you, accessed June 10, 2013.

2. For more information on the TED Fellows Program, visit www.ted.com/fellows.

3. John Rockwell, "One of the Deadly Sins, and a Conundrum Too," *New York Times*, December 21, 2006.

http://www.nytimes.com/2006/12/21/arts/dance/21move.html
?_r=0, accessed June 10, 2013.

Patterns

1. Daniel Smith, *Monkey Mind: A Memoir of Anxiety* (New York: Simon & Shuster, 2012), page 89.

Power

1. Lisa Nichols comment in a webinar in 2012.

INDEX OF PEOPLE

A

Auerbach, Red ix
Anderson, Kevin J. 12, 197
Ardagh, Arjuna 166
Arnoudse, Don 20, 40, 166, 191

B

Baryshnikov 134
Begley, Chris 44, 45, 47
Bennett, Nigel 13–18
Blanchard, Madeleine Homan 105, 140, 155, 192
Boothroyd, David 76, 78, 191
Bragar, Dr. Joan 115, 167, 191
Brock, Dr. Vikki ix

C

Cappellino, Mark 19, 41, 48, 117, 191
Clinton, Hillary 121, 198
Cohen, Jennifer 29, 40, 166, 191
Confucius 1, 131, 197, 198
Cooper, Dr. Marc 61, 113, 115, 128, 189, 191

D

Dalgas, Gini 82–88
DiBianca, Vince 74, 139, 150, 152, 153, 191
Disraeli, Benjamin 22, 197

E

Edwards, Dr. Mary 77, 192

F

Field, Patricia 134
Forst, Judith 69–74, 197–198
Freedman, Renee 62, 64, 66, 192
Fullerton, Dr. Rick 52, 189, 192

G

Gallwey, Tim ix
Garn, James R. 114, 165, 192
Graham, Martha 132

H

Hawley, Nancy Miriam 28, 192
Hayford, Coach Jim 33–38, 40–41
Henderson, Allan 53, 79, 192
Hendrickson, Dr. Carolyn 50, 90, 192
Herbert, Brian 12, 197
Hill, Napoleon 94, 198

J

Jacks, Lawrence Pearsall 43, 197
Jamison, Victoria 23–28
Jung, Carl 54, 197

L

LaRoche, Gina 65, 193
Laveman, Dave 153, 193
Lawrence, Kevin 18, 20, 193
Leech, Ryan 89, 92, 102, 119, 129, 193
Lo, Dr. John C. 122–127, 129
Loop, Kim 102, 116, 180, 193

M

Majer, Chris 10, 38, 163, 193
Martin, Marcia 75, 78, 104, 116, 185, 193
McCuaig, Leslie 170–177
McDermott, Michael 65, 101, 193
Move, Richard 132–137, 198

N

Nichols, Lisa 168, 199

P

Paolo 4–10, 21, 46

R

Ramachandra, Sumant 44–48, 72
Ray, Michael 81, 88, 198
Rhoads, Virginia 91, 92, 104, 129, 194
Roddick, Anita 106

Rosen, Michael 108–113
Rundle, Denise 95–100, 102, 170

S

Seeton, Tim 91, 101, 113, 130, 194
Selman, Jim xi, 2, 107, 115, 120, 189, 194
Shaked, Anabella 30, 103, 115, 194
Smith, Charles E. 63, 116, 117, 138, 151, 164, 179, 183, 194
Smith, Daniel 142, 199

T

Tucker, Leslie 49, 68, 179, 194

V

Van Note, Jill 114, 195
van Schaayk, Frank 143–150

W

Weaver, David 55–60
Williams, Val 118, 178, 195
Wooden, John ix, 32, 197

Y

Young, Jonathan 185

Z

Zesbaugh, Mark 157–162

ABOUT THE AUTHOR

Shae Hadden is a writer, writing coach, and communications consultant. She partners with leaders, executive coaches, and leadership development experts to help them effectively engage people in creating positive, sustainable change.

Shae pays forward the contributions of all her coaches with this book. She can be reached at shaehadden.com.

Made in the USA
Charleston, SC
04 September 2014